THE BEAT ON WESTER

(A Celebration of 150 years
of the Policing of Tavistock)

with best wishes

By SIMON DELL, MBE

FOREST PUBLISHING

(In association with the Devon & Cornwall Constabulary)

First published in 1997 by FOREST PUBLISHING (in association with the Devon & Cornwall Constabulary), Woodstock, Liverton, Newton Abbot, Devon TQ12 6JJ

British Library Cataloguing in Publication Data

A catalogue record for this book is available from the British Library.

ISBN 0–9527297–4–1

Forest Publishing

Editorial by:
Wendy Roderick Hake

Design and layout by:
Mike Lang

Typeset by:
Carnaby Typesetting, Torquay, Devon TQ1 1EG

Printed and bound in Great Britain by:
BPC Wheatons Ltd., Exeter, Devon EX2 8RP

Cover photographs:

Front –	*(Top)*	Sergeant Bob Thomas outside Tavistock police station c1949.
	(Centre)	The Duke of Bedford's statue – Guildhall Square, Tavistock c1895.
	(Lower)	Sergeant Gale, with three constables (George Marshall of Whitchurch on right), outside Tavistock police station on 9th August 1930.
Back –		The author on duty beside the River Tavy, 1981

Jim Thorrington

DEDICATION

This book is dedicated to
those whose commitment to duty has created
one of the finest of British institutions

The Office of Constable

Outside Princetown police house 1946. Inspector Turner of Tavistock with Sergeant Perryman of
Lifton, Constable Tancock of Princetown and Motor Patrol Constable Scoble of Tavistock.
Ret'd Ch/Supt R. Perryman

In the hope that the passage of time and progress
will not destroy its dignity and tradition

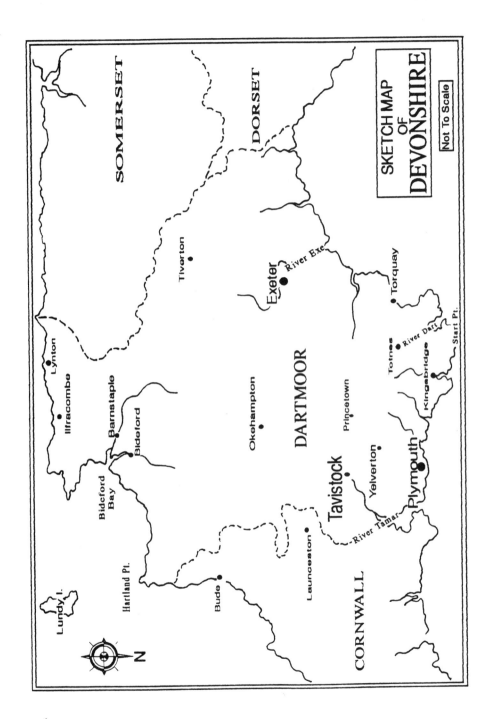

SKETCH MAP
OF
DEVONSHIRE

Not To Scale

SOMERSET

DORSET

Tiverton

River Exe

Exeter

Torquay

Lynton

River Dart

Ilfracombe

Totnes

Start Pt.

Barnstaple

Kingsbridge

Bideford

DARTMOOR

Okehampton

Princetown

Plymouth

Bideford
Bay

Yelverton

Tavistock

River Tamar

Launceston

Hartland Pt.

Lundy I.

Bude

CORNWALL

N

4

CONTENTS

(Note: The numbers in brackets which appear within the text of this book refer to the main sources of reference as listed in the bibliography).

ACKNOWLEDGEMENTS

Such a book would be impossible to research and produce without the support and assistance of many people, far and wide. Retired police officers, too many to count, have had the tables of time turned upon them. They have been subjected to the most intense of grillings and interviews. Their private photograph albums have been ransacked without complaint, for it is they who made this history and are a living part of it. To those many I give my thanks. To the widows, sons and daughters of officers long since gone, I am grateful; for their understanding and wish to record duties performed so many years ago, for their desire, like mine, not to see that history goes untold.

To the Chief Constable, John Evans, whose permission and support provided the foundation and motivation for this book. I trust that it does not disappoint him.

To former Superintendent Derek Roper, whose family connections with the Devon Constabulary and the police service go back to their origins and beyond, and to Brian Phillips, whose memorable contribution to policing commenced in the Tavistock area and concluded as Assistant Chief Constable, but whose ties with West Devon were never forgotten.

My gratitude goes to retired Constable Ken Northey of Tavistock. His ability to recall faces and names of half a century ago made the identification of photographs an easy one. And to his wife, Georgina, who, like the constables' wives of her generation, never thought of complaining at dirty police boots in her house, wet helmets on her dining room table and tea drunk into the early hours, whilst past deeds of unrepeatable mischief were recounted and recorded!

To Graham Kirkpatrick, stalwart of Tavistock Museum, for his patient support and research on my behalf; Trevor James, author, of South Zeal for his encouragement and guiding hand, and to Helen Joy Harris, author and historian, for editorial assistance and historical facts. My thanks also to the archivist of the Police Museum, Brian Estill, whose interest in the most obscure of questions was remarkable; and to Gerry Woodcock, local historian and author of many books on the subject of Tavistock, for allowing me to share a wealth of his material, researched over many years.

To the many people of West Devon and beyond, who have let me into their homes to discuss and record the most seemingly insignificant of detail that proved so important in the history of the policing of West Devon. To Jim Thorrington, photographer and great friend and neighbour of policemen for almost half a century, my thanks for the many photographs in this book that he took, and for his encouragement and inspiration to record such a history.

To Wendy Roderick Hake for editing this book whilst still finding the time to look after a young family and be in a full-time teaching job at Tavistock College. Her patience translated my notes into the English language! – I owe her so much. To Pete Myatt, community photographer of Tavistock, for his photographic expertise and enthusiasm; and to my young friend, David Pithouse, for his help in printing my manuscripts. To the many serving officers who, themselves, belong to families with generations of police service. It is they, whose efforts are a fine tribute to their fathers and beyond, who strive to uphold the traditions that have made the Office of Constable an honourable one.

And, finally, to those closest to me who never joined the police service, but became as much a part of it as I. To those who tolerate the intrusions into a home that befalls the duties of a constable. To whom the public turn for a source of advice and support when I am not there. To whom the role of community policeman would be made impossible without their support – my family. Thank you Shirley, Matthew and Laura.

❃ ❃ ❃ ❃ ❃

AUTHOR'S NOTE

Whilst every care has been taken in preparing this book, it is only reasonable that the effects of time and human frailty should be taken into account. If a name is spelt or recalled incorrectly then an apology is offered in advance. Where an opinion is expressed, it is that of the author and not of the Devon & Cornwall Constabulary.

Whilst the Devon & Cornwall Constabulary hold the copyright to this publication, Constable Simon Dell exercises his right to be known as 'The Author'. The author receives no monies from the sales of this book. The editor, Wendy Roderick Hake, gave her services voluntarily, as did Helen Joy Harris.

Any profits from the sale of this book are to be donated to the 'Flint House' Police Convalescent Home appeal fund charity.

❃ ❃ ❃ ❃ ❃

FOREWORD

The Chief Constable.

A celebration of 150 years of service is a worthy milestone in any organisation. When the anniversary to be celebrated is for a police station that is rare indeed, and the Devon & Cornwall Constabulary is proud to be associated so closely with such a celebration for one of its own stations. The modern police service is constantly under pressure to adapt to meet changes in the demands made by society, this book celebrates one and a half centuries of such change as we strive continually to provide a service second to none. Tavistock Police Station has been a constant home to its Parish Force, the Devon County Constabulary and latterly the Devon & Cornwall Constabulary, throughout that time since 1848, ranking it amongst one of the oldest police stations in the country. To glance through these pages is to step back in time and share in the pride of the many officers who have served Tavistock and the communities of West Devon through those years.

This is an excellent piece of research by a working police officer with an obvious passion for Tavistock, in which he is so well known and respected. The enormous amount of effort the production has taken is a tribute to his love of his work and his town. The credit belongs entirely to him.

John Evans O.St.J Q.P.M. LLB
Chief Constable
Police Headquarters
Exeter
June 1997

9

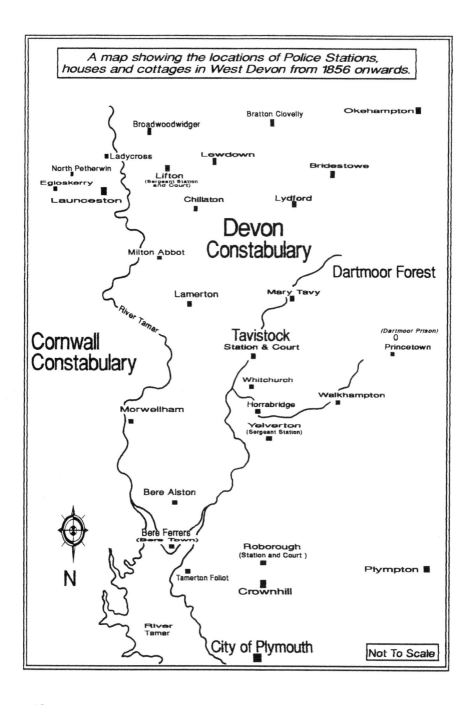

A map showing the locations of Police Stations, houses and cottages in West Devon from 1856 onwards.

Okehampton

Bratton Clovelly

Broadwoodwidger

Ladycross

Lewdown

Bridestowe

North Petherwin

Lifton
(Sergeant Station and Court)

Egloskerry

Launceston

Chillaton

Lydford

Devon
Constabulary

Milton Abbot

Dartmoor Forest

Lamerton

Mary Tavy

River Tamar

Cornwall
Constabulary

Tavistock
Station & Court

(Dartmoor Prison)
0
Princetown

Whitchurch

Walkhampton

Morwellham

Horrabridge

Yelverton
(Sergeant Station)

Bere Alston

N

Bere Ferrers
(Bere Town)

Roborough
(Station and Court)

Plympton

Tamerton Foliot

Crownhill

River
Tamar

City of Plymouth

Not To Scale

INTRODUCTION

Like some phoenix rising from the ashes, Tavistock guildhall and police station were built from the ruinous and dilapidated fragments of the old Abbey of Tavistock, long since demolished at the behest of Henry VIII. On 28th September 1848, at the instigation and generosity of the Duke of Bedford, a new guildhall was opened. Designed by the Plymouth architect John Foulston and constructed for the occupancy and work of the local Justices of the Peace, the parish police service and the fire brigade, little did the duke envisage that his magnificent building would be used for that purpose one and a half centuries later.

An 18th century print of the ruinous Tavistock Abbey.

Robin Fenner

It is that 150 years of unique history that this book commemorates. Only a few other police stations in Great Britain can boast a longer occupancy, and even then it is only by months and not decades. Tavistock police station, the oldest still in constant use in the westcountry, was built to house the parish police force, prior to the Devon Constabulary's birth in 1856. Although the fire station has long since been moved to more modern premises, the police and magistrates still enjoy the occupancy of one of the most ornate and historical buildings in the town, if not the county. Policemen have come and gone, deeds humourous and dastardly have shaken the fabric of the building. But, throughout all this, it has stood the march of time, and looks set to do so for many more years. Its future surely depends upon those in positions of authority, so long as they can see progress and efficiency, modernisation and computerisation being compatible with the traditions of the police service. Both, it is certain, can run hand in hand if we do but let them, to the benefit of all whom the police strive to serve.

If only its granite steps, worn by the boots of many hundreds of constables, could tell the tales of what they had seen ... One thing would be for sure, it would be a story of pride and tradition, of service tinged, no doubt, with a quiet tear from the toughest of men. It would, almost certainly, be a story that few police stations can boast. The many police houses and cottages of yesteryear, coming under the jurisdiction of Tavistock, are recounted. They are treated with as much importance as the guildhall itself. For it was the constables of those stations who played such a vital part in this, the story of policing in the Tavistock and West Devon area. This small book hopes to tell but a fragment of that story: 150 years cannot be told in these few pages. Much, therefore, has to be left unsaid – for the moment. If this story leaves you wondering at the hardships and privations of our constabulary forebears, if it leaves you with a sense of gratitude for their efforts and a pride that the British police service is without equal anywhere, then the story was worth telling.

SIMON P. DELL, MBE
Police Constable
Tavistock
June 1997

❋ ❋ ❋ ❋ ❋

Chapter 1

EARLY YEARS

(Policing medieval Tavistock)

The Metropolitan Police, formed in 1829 by Sir Robert Peel, was a leading example of a modern police force. It was, however, to be some time before Sir Robert's example was followed in the counties of England, especially in the lower populated ones where the long-established provincial system of locally-appointed men seemed adequate for the needs of the less informed and poorly educated majority. Indeed, it was to be another 28 years after the streets of London saw the first peeler that the lanes and tracks of rural Devon echoed to the boots of the local, full-time, paid constable. Then, at long last, came the turning point in the administration of law and order throughout the county: men would now be properly equipped and trained for their duties. Marching many miles on their often mundane beats, their appointments slung in bags on their backs, these men proved to be the mainstay in the fight against crime and disorder.

It was the forerunners of these men of the then new Devon Constabulary who upheld the ancient office of policemanship. Poorly educated, with little or no training for their many responsibilities, they were nominated by a local parish committee, each being known as a 'Parish Constable'. His authority extended throughout the parish, but he received no salary, relying, instead, upon a regular occupation, or trade, to earn his livelihood, and was able only to claim certain expenses. As a result, it is hardly surprising to learn that it was not always a popular appointment. Yet, in spite of this, there are many instances of reselections taking place several times over. In fact, whilst some new names do appear each year in the registers, there are others that recur year after year – clearly the duties of these men in the preceding 12 months had met with the approval of the local Justice of the Peace, upon whose authority they acted and whose agents they were! It needs also to be mentioned that having been appointed by the local magistrate (usually for a year at a time) the authority bestowed upon them was obviously a measure of trust, commanding a degree of respect.

A quiet rural parish would invariably appoint just two such custodians

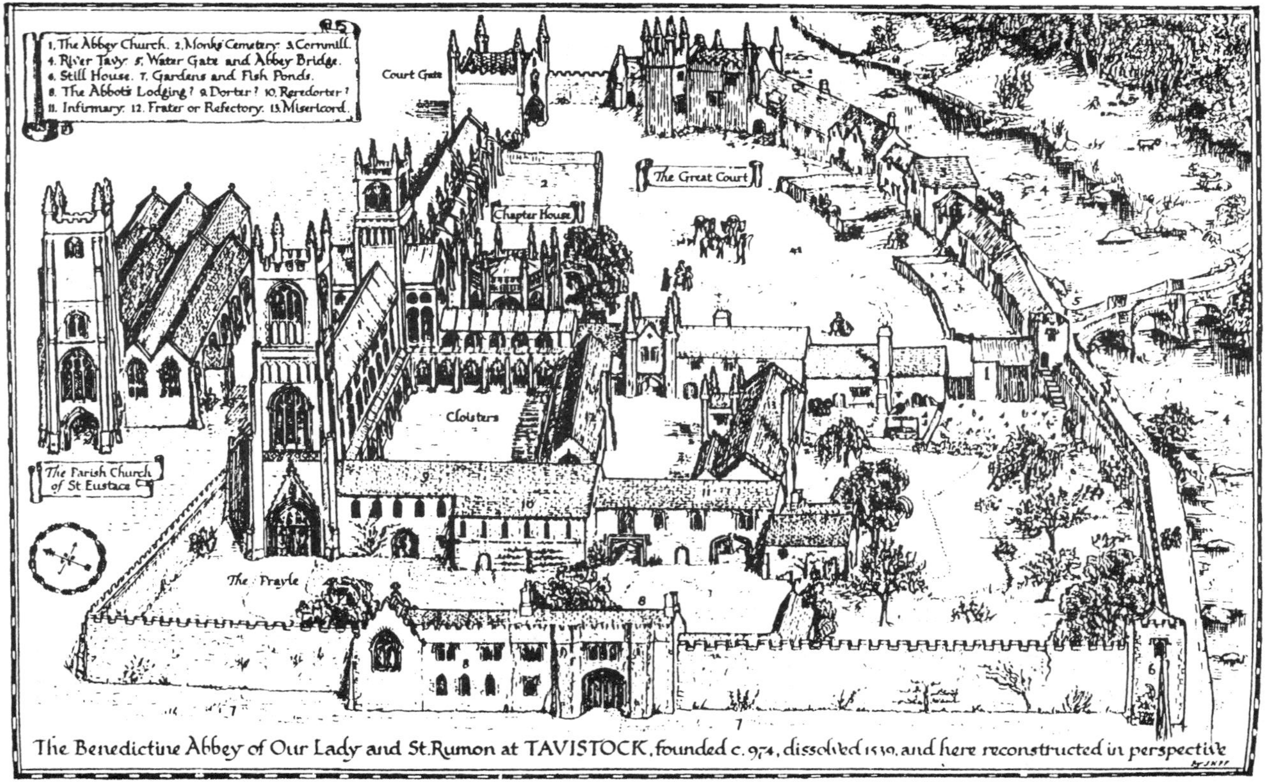

The Benedictine Abbey of Our Lady and St. Rumon at TAVISTOCK, founded c. 974, dissolved 1539, and here reconstructed in perspective.

Key (within the illustration):
1. The Abbey Church. 2. Monks' Cemetery. 3. Cornmill. 4. River Tavy. 5. Water Gate and Abbey Bridge. 6. Still House. 7. Gardens and Fish Ponds. 8. The Abbot's Lodging. 9. a Dorter. 10. Reredorter. 11. Infirmary. 12. Frater or Refectory. 13. Misericord.

Court Gate

The Great Court

Cloisters

The Dayle

The Parish Church of St Eustace

An impression of Tavistock Abbey drawn by H.P.R. Finberg.

From 'Tavistock Abbey' (David & Charles, 1969), by kind permission of the publishers of the peace, but in the larger parish of Tavistock four were usually appointed. However, in busy years, when the populace was troublesome, up to eight or nine officers were known to have held office as parish constable. When making such appointments in Tavistock, the magistrates would obviously take consideration of local feelings and the opinion of the town's elders. The influence of His Grace The Duke of Bedford would never be too far away either, and there would be an almost automatic approval of any suggestion of an appointment that came from his direction. Such was the way of tradition, and so had it been for several hundred years.

To go any further back into the origins of the police force, locally, we would need to travel all the way in history to the 'Tithingman' of the Middle Ages. The territorial divisions of policing at that time were variously known by many names, including 'Hundred'. The first statutory mention of the word 'Constable' is in 1252: the derivation of the term is generally regarded as being 'Comes Stabuli' – master of the horse. In England, at this time, every male person, unless excused by high office or social position, was enrolled for police purposes. They would serve in a group of about ten families known as a tithing and be headed by a Tithingman, each man being responsible for the behaviour of his neighbours. Groups of tithings were formed into hundreds, with the Hundred Man exercising administrative power through the Hundred Court.

The next milestone in law enforcement was the Statute of Winchester of 1285. It is here that the foundations of our modern-day neighbourhood watch schemes were laid. Residents kept 'Watch and Ward', with every man between the ages of fifteen and sixty duty-bound to keep arms available to uphold the laws. One of the two High Constables of the Hundred would inspect such arms twice a year.

The Statute of Winchester was the only piece of legislation relating to the policing of the country for almost 600 years, until the Metropolitan Police Act of 1829. It is, therefore, quite understandable that such change would be met with suspicion and mistrust by the public. For centuries they had been governed by a system of policing in West Devon based upon the Borough Court or, as it was more commonly known, the 'Shammel-Moot'. This court was influenced by the great power of the Abbot of Tavistock. Indeed, the power of life and death lay in his hands. In the field, known on the 19th century maps as 'Forges Field', beside the road at Pitland, near Lamerton, the Abbot had his gallows(10). Like any other lord, he held his court governing the lives of those beholding to him. Incidentally, the hill at Mary Tavy, on the main road north to Okehampton, called Gibbet Hill gets its name from the 'gibbet' of the Middle Ages. This stood at the junction of the track near to where the cattle grid used to be at the top of the hill leading out of the village. The gibbet was an iron cage used to display a corpse cut from the gallows as a deterrent to the would-be footpad or plunderer. The unlucky highwayman might even be sentenced live to the gibbet. There he remained until his demise, sometimes prolonged by the well meaning efforts of passers-by, who might provide him with water

Inevitably, the advent of the Justice of the Peace degraded the constable's office, but even so it was slow to lose its feudal dignity. During the 15th and much of the 16th centuries he was still pre-eminent amongst the four principal annually elected officers of the parish, these being constable, churchwarden, surveyor of the highways and overseer of the poor. He held this position in some small towns such as Tavistock until the 18th and early parts of the 19th centuries. To understand why many bought their way out of serving as parish constable, a formerly honourable office, one must look at the great commitments he faced, his work taking much of the time that he could have spent making profit from his regular employment. A constable's duties were based upon common law but were extended, latterly, by Parliament. The oath taken locally by the parish constables read thus(1):–

"You shall swear that you shall keep the peace of our Lord the King well, and lawfully according to your powers, and shall arrest all those who shall make any contest, riot, debate or affray, in breaking of the said peace, and shall bring them into the house or Compter of one of the Sheriffs. And if you shall be withstood by strength of such misdooers, you shall raise upon them hue and cry, and shall follow them from street to street and from ward to ward until they are arrested. And you shall search at all times when you shall be required by scavenger or bedel, for the common nuisances of the ward, until they are arrested ... and the faults you shall find, you shall present them unto the Mayor and to the offices of the said town ... so God help you and the Saints."

In practice this meant that the constable had to set the nightly watch in the town. He would take over prisoners from the watchmen and place them in the stocks, or lock-up. In many instances he would keep them in his own cottage until he was able to deliver them to a Justice of the Peace. The stocks of Tavistock are now in the museum after being retrieved from neglect in the old police cells. They used to stand at the foot of Kilworthy Hill near the point where the Ordulph Arms now stands. With his staff of office in his hand, the constable was to initiate the 'hue and cry'. This was a document that since the 18th century has been known as a warrant. His staff, or baton, was his symbol of authority, which might have hung outside his cottage door. It was often ornately decorated, and there are many fine examples, such as those of the Tavistock parish constables and the rural 'Beerferris' parish constable, available to be seen. The staff was also available as a defensive weapon, yet the constable wore no distinctive uniform of any kind.

With the dissolution of the monasteries in the time of Henry VIII, a great number of vagrants emerged in the area. Their only alternative to

Three examples of the truncheons used by Tavistock parish constables. *Left to right:* a Victorian truncheon (1842), a George IV Tavistock borough police tipstaff (1800) and a Victorian truncheon (c1845).

Courtesy of Tavistock Museum

starvation was theft. Under the barbaric laws of the Tudors, the parish constable was the principal agent in dealing out punishment before whipping the vagabond out of the town. The parish constable was under a legal obligation to bring before the court leet which appointed him, latterly called the court of quarter sessions, reports about those who had offended against the laws. This ancient system has seen little change with the passing of centuries.

As the first few years of the 19th century passed, growing discontent to the manner in which the country was policed created a great need for reform. Times were changing quickly! The Napoleonic wars and the social unrest that followed made greater demands for a more efficient way of policing an ever-growing and troublesome population. The system that had existed for hundreds of years was slowly crumbling.

Many parishes, locally, might still have been pleased with the continued efforts of their parochially appointed law-men. Proof enough of this satisfaction came in 1830. The five local constables of Tavistock were awarded a £1 bonus for their diligence in apprehending two notorious burglars named Drew and Marchall. But, in line with the general discontent throughout the country, the Duke of Bedford's agent, one Andrew Wilson, complained thus:-

"The state of the police of the town is a most crying evil. It is needless, however to complain of them. They are too imbecile to be made of any use."

It was Mr Wilson's successor, as agent of the Duke, John Benson, who continued the attack. He proclaimed that "they contrive to be drunk a great part of their time". The townspeople followed the assault upon these well meaning officers with their own complaints:-

"The constables have been very negligent in visiting the public houses on the Sabbath day, particularly during divine service, and not dispersing those parties that are assembled in the streets."

※ ※ ※ ※ ※

Chapter 2

MERRITT'S MEN

In 1837 the duke's agent, John Benson, took the extraordinary step of calling in the Metropolitan Police. Tavistock was to borrow two of their officers to visit the town in order to give advice and direction, and to provide a degree of training to the local officers. Benson later wrote – "We have got the London policemen and already find a benefit." By the end of the year the successes of this initiative were clearly recognised and the suggestions of the peelers had been implemented: the parish had appointed its first full-time, paid professional chief of police, one Superintendent Mark Merritt. He was ensconced, by the parish, in the old guildhall building in Bedford Square and, once there, began to organise the duties of his unpaid and locally appointed rag-bag of non-permanent officers. For such duties, he received 25 shillings a week. But he, too, was appointed each year in the spring by the annual vestry meetings and confirmed in his duties by the local Justice of the Peace. Although great advances had been made, there were still the vestiges of the old system to be discarded. Meanwhile, Superintendent Merritt remained in post for 20 years, his pay unchanging in all that time, although by 1842 he had been joined by John Physick, another paid and full-time officer.

John Physick had split duties, his time being spent between acting as Superintendent Merritt's deputy and, when required, the 'Union Clerk' and 'Superintendent Registrar' for the town. His pay, reflecting his position as deputy, amounted to 19 shillings a week and he, too, remained in office until the station in the community was replaced by the new Devon County Constabulary in 1857.

The local Tavistock Parish Police was regarded sufficiently worthy of mention in the 1844 *General Police and Constabulary List* (a quarterly publication of criminal and police statistics). It refers to the Superintendent as being Mr Mark Merritt, appointed in 1837 and with his central office at the Guildhall, his assistant officer, being Mr J. Physick. On top of his police duties, Mr Merritt is recorded as being the Inspector of the Fire-Engine Establishment, having been appointed in that same year of 1837. Yet he is shown as being the deputy to the Chief Manager, Mr William Monk, who had been appointed some 9 years previously in

Tavistock Abbey buildings before restoration, 1833.
Robin Fenner

1828. The almanac goes on to detail that "Two engines at chief station, Bedford Square, and a fire escape at Market House, worked by the constables and supernumeraries." The fire engine room, with its great oak doors, has since been converted to offices and stores, a more mundane function akin to modern policing requirements.

The uniform of the Tavistock Parish Police in 1844 consisted of a blue coat with white embroidery and buttons, their jurisdiction being the Borough of Tavistock with a population of 6,000. The civil authorities at the time were 'The Boroughreeve', John Geddy Mitchell Esq., and the 'High Constable', Mr Chubb. The criminal statistics of 1844 would be the envy of their modern-day counterparts 150 years later. With eleven petty and two serious misdemeanours for the quarter, life in the parish police could hardly be regarded as hectic. The nine recorded felonies, totalling a cost of two pounds and fifteen shillings worth of stolen goods, resulted in a detection rate that was most creditable. Having recovered all but 18 shillings worth of the property within a few weeks, the parish force would have been regarded well. The almanac for 1844 shows that their attention was not only turned towards the rising trend in criminal activities, though. That year their good officers saved the life of one town resident, and this is duly recorded with distinction.

By 1850 Mr John Crossman had joined Messrs Merritt and Physick as the third paid officer of the local police, their combined presence being accepted as part of the life of the town. Their role as professional police officers overseeing their unpaid parish constables had become formalised as an official institution. An Act of Parliament in 1842 turned its attention to the conscripted parish constables and the system by which they were engaged and treated. It was a time of consolidation and progress into a more accepted and formal style of policing. This Act, no doubt to the delight of these poorly rewarded officers, laid down a standard scale of allowances for their duties. The service of a summons attracted the payment of a shilling, and the execution of a warrant brought the appealing sum of 2 shillings. If the constable was involved in the searching of a public house or attending a public meeting the princely sum of half a crown could be claimed. The officer was entitled to claim a supplement of 3 pence per mile for distances travelled on duty. At last, the previously unpaid and ill-treated parish constable could look upon his duties with a little more interest. The other formalised change brought about by the 1842 Act was far-reaching. Every able-bodied resident of the parish between the ages of twenty-five and fifty-five were now liable for conscripted service as a parish constable.

The candidate had to be one who paid a certain level of local property tax. Few men fitting such criteria could expect to be missed by the committee who nominated constables to the Justices for approval. That is, of course, unless his name managed to get its way on to the numerous lists of exemptions which existed. These lists of candidates for appointment were prepared by the annual parish vestry meetings, the vestry comprising representatives of the local ratepayers. They left off the names of exempted men, or those who had already done their year's service, and were thus excused from reappointment. These lists were then conveyed to the magistrates at the Tavistock court, where the Justices would make deliberations as to how many constables would need to be appointed for the following year. If a certain individual was chosen, he could try to find a substitute to replace him if he was so against the idea of serving as constable. In the first year of the new Act, the Tavistock parish vestry meeting put the names of 15 men forward to the Justices as individuals who would appear suitable to fulfil the role. Henceforth, each year a similar sized list was forwarded for consideration. And each year the three paid officials, Merritt, Physick and, from 1850, Crossman, would be included in those named.

From that list of fifteen, the three paid officers were reselected each year, along with six unpaid constables. By 1845 the number had increased to seven constables, then to ten in 1849. Again, it increased to eleven in 1851, taking account of the increase in population in the town in the previous 10 years. The three paid officers were reselected each year as a matter of course, it seems. Also appointed regularly were parish constables John Algar, a dealer in game, Walter Reddicliffe, a farmer, and John Cerutty and William Dyer – both bakers in the town. We can only assume that they were content with their service to the town and that their seniors were content with their conduct and duties. Such sentiments were clearly not shared by Simon Westcott, a draper, and Thomas Palmer, a currier, who paid others to take their places on the vestry nomination.

Chapter 3

A GUILDHALL FROM A GENEROUS DUKE

(The new Tavistock guildhall is built)

Tavistock police station and court, c1890.
Robin Fenner

Superintendent Merritt and his men's former headquarters was in the old guildhall in Bedford Square. This had been described as a "one-roomed inconveniently constructed building". It was situated in the remains of the old abbey ruins and had been the home for the court since the 16th century. Superintendent Merritt shared his accommodation with the Clerk to the Justices, who went so far in 1845 as to say that the building was "in a very dilapidated state". The Duke of Bedford, as was often the case, looked favourably upon the plight of the police and Justices. From the ruins of the old abbey buildings in 1848 rose a new and magnificent guildhall. Replacing the old and 'dilapidated' building, it has from that time provided a joint home for both the court and the police, in addition

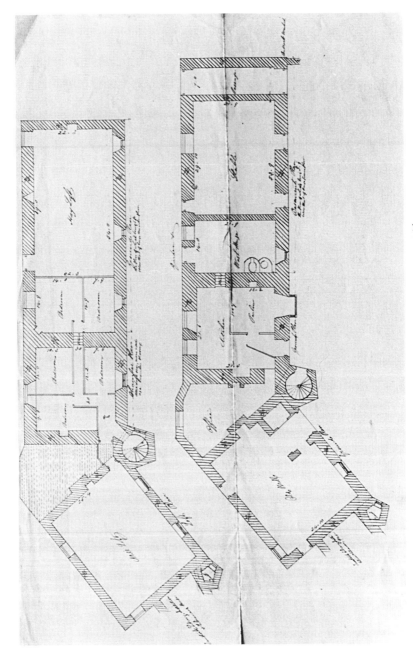

A plan of Tavistock guildhall square buildings before restoration, 1846.
Courtesy of Tavistock Museum

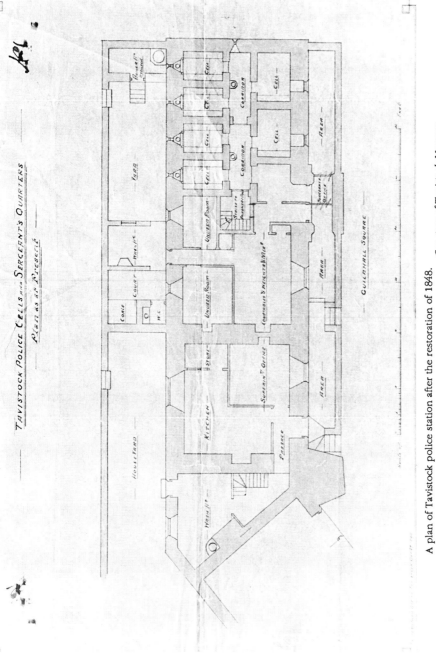

A plan of Tavistock police station after the restoration of 1848. *Courtesy of Tavistock Museum*

to serving, briefly, as a headquarters for the town's fire brigade. Opened on September 28th that year, it has stood the test of time to become one of the oldest, continually used buildings to house a police force in Great Britain.

The *Sherborne and Yeovil Mercury*(9) of Saturday 7th October 1848 proudly declared to its readers:–

"A new Guildhall has been erected at Tavistock by the Duke of Bedford. Its site is where a portion of the Abbey once stood. Adjoining the venerable remains of the once monastic Chapel. The Duke has also recently drained the town in the most complete style by efficient sewerage and supplied its inhabitants with a never failing stream of excellent water."

The erection of the guildhall was just one example of the great

Tavistock magistrates court, 1994.
Author's collection

undertaking of reconstruction of the town by His Grace, Francis, the 7th Duke of Bedford. John Foulston, the Plymouth architect, was engaged for the purpose by the duke. Foulston provided what must have been regarded as palatial accommodation for the police in comparison with their ruinous and humble building. The use of local stone and reclaimed granite from the old abbey ruins ensured that the great differences in age between the existing buildings and the new guildhall was hardly noticeable.

The guildhall comprised an ornately decorated courtroom with heraldic coats of arms of the Sovereign, the Duke of Cornwall and the Duke of Bedford adorning the walls. Along with the statue of 'Justice', the duke certainly intended his court to be fit for the visiting Justices of the quarter sessions courts. With the reorganisation of the justice system, the facilities are now used as a magistrates court. Held every Friday, it still upholds an important function in the judicial life of West Devon. Below the courtrooms was situated the accommodation for the parish police force with its bridewell consisting of seven cells directly beneath the dock of the court. A narrow stairway led from the cells up into the dock, a stairway which has seen numerous scuffles with reluctant prisoners! A guardroom for the constables and an office for the superintendent occupied the lower ground floor area. A spiral stairway led up and across into the private quarters attached to the station.

The town's fire engine was housed in the large room with double doors at the front of the building. A fire grate was kept burning with coals to transfer into the firebox of the steam-powered water pump on the engine. The motive power was supplied by horses which were stabled at the building now known as The Bedford Hotel. An ornate gas lamp stood outside of the 'fire engine station' and a large notice hung above the doors explaining how to summon the services of the fire brigade. Mr George Merrifield, being the superintendent of the service, had a band of unpaid volunteers to carry out fire-fighting duties in the parish and beyond. They were called to duty by the sound of the single tenor bell rung from the church tower opposite. How effective this early fire brigade was remains shrouded in mystery, but reports of cottages and houses in the outlying villages being burned to the ground before the slow arrival of the horse-drawn fire engine abound. They remained in this home until being moved, along with their motor-powered engine, into the building now used as the town's library. Keen to preserve tradition, the fire service personnel posed for photographs outside their ancestral home for many years until the 1960s. It was only then, after an untimely and accidental sounding of the engine's emergency bell, that they decided to find a more convenient location. Perhaps the police sergeant's wife trying to get their children to sleep might have influenced the decision – we will never know!

This new guildhall must have improved the morale of the police

The old cells of Tavistock police station, 1994.

Author's collection

service and their supervisors immensely. Moving from their dilapidated and unsatisfactory rooms that they once occupied to an ornate, purpose-built station, must also have seemed progress beyond belief. Little could they have realised that one and a half centuries later their successors would still be functioning in the same building. The interior has long since been modernised and expanded, the requirements of a modern-day police force being much more demanding than those of their predecessors. But, throughout these changes, the building, outwardly, retained its original facade. The duke had ensured that the new guildhall would blend in with the older buildings surrounding Court Gate. And his architect, Foulston, had been blessed with foresight ahead of his time, it seems. The use of old granite, stones and window mullions made certain that the guildhall matched the nearby tower and archway perfectly; little would the visitor realise that several hundred years exist between the various parts of the building.

The tower building contains a fine spiral stairway which, unlike its military counterpart, winds anti-clockwise, a sign of ecclesiastical use. The military stairways, on the other hand, wound in the opposite direction so as to prevent use of the favoured right arm for wielding the sword of an attacking aggressor. Although never designed for fortification, this is the one part of the building which survived the ravages of Henry VIII.

The spiral stairway leads up to the present-day magistrates' retiring room, an area once occupied by bedrooms of long ago. It is said that a judge by the name of 'Trout' lived in this part of the ruinous remains of the old abbey centuries ago. His reputation, like his successor, Judge Jefferies, was a formidable one. A visit on night shift by a newly appointed recruit usually guaranteed an ashen-faced young constable by the morning for Judge Trout's house has never been the place to be in the quiet, early hours, when the building creaks and groans at the stories its walls hide!

✻ ✻ ✻ ✻ ✻

Chapter 4

THE UNPAID PROFESSIONAL

(The village parish constable)

Tavistock was, and still is, a town in the middle of a great rural area of West Devon. In the 19th century it included nine principal parishes, those of Bere Ferrers, Brentor, Lamerton, Lydford, Mary Tavy, Milton Abbot, Peter Tavy, Sampford Spiney and Whitchurch. They, too, had their parish vestry meetings and submitted the names of nominated parishioners to the Tavistock court for consideration for service as constable. Their parish constables were appointed having regard to the population of the parish. Between 1840 and 1850, Brentor, Lydford, Milton Abbot, Peter Tavy and Sampford Spiney had two constables appointed in each parish. Lamerton, being a more populated area, had three officers appointed. But the likes of Mary Tavy, with its many mines and industries, needed a minimum of four officers to contain the rowdyism and crime wave of the area. The parish vestry meeting at Lamerton on 1st April 1852 put forward the names of eight suitable candidates for the Justices to choose their three officers from:-

John Percy	of Lamerton	a Registrar
William Brook	of Whitslade	a Yeoman
William Percy	of Meadwell	a Yeoman
Arthur Stanbury	of Woodly	a Yeoman
Samuel Paler	of Trevenn	a Yeoman
William Rice	of North Brentor	a Blacksmith
William Brook	of South Brentor	a Yeoman
John Williams	of Woodmanswell	a Yeoman

(The term Yeoman referred to a freehold, middle-class farmer or small estate owner of the parish.)

In the parish of Whitchurch the number of parish constables was increased, in 1848, from two to three. By way of contrast, Bere Ferrers needed, it was considered, eight or nine appointed officers to effectively uphold the law. It was certainly one of the largest parishes in the area, covering the whole of the Bere peninsular, including Bere Alston village and the many mines that were in operation at that time. The spring vestry meetings, producing its annual lists, usually nominated about twice the amount of candidates for the final required number of constables. Although some parishes, like Mary Tavy in 1848, nominated just the right amount for the positions required, they must have been confident in their nominees. The Justices, however, would not have looked favourably upon such impertinence. They, no doubt, liked to exercise their powers of discretion in having a choice to make in their appointments, so being presented with such a *fait-accompli* would almost certainly have displeased them somewhat. The meetings of these local committees were known as the vestry meetings, their name being taken from the vestry of the local parish church, where the meetings were usually held. However, towards the middle of the 19th century, the Edgecombe Arms in Bere Alston seems to have been the favoured place for the vestry committee of that parish to hold their gathering. These committees tended to be quite small affairs considering the importance of the issues that they were deciding upon. There would surely have been reason enough to attend the vestry if only to ensure your name did not find its way to the Justices in Tavistock!

The local overseer of the poor of the parish would check the list and sign it in order that it might be duly presented for consideration by the magistrates. He would commence by stating "...that the following persons be returned as fit to act as constables...". The overseer of the parish of Brentor must surely have become acquainted with the name of Elias Tooker of that parish. He was a man who was reappointed for 20 years without a break. Likewise was the case in Mary Tavy parish, where John Down regularly appears as constable. In both Peter Tavy and Bere Ferrers parishes the same situation occurred. Peter Holmes and William Langman's names respectively reappeared year after year as the men chosen by their parish's vestry meetings. The vestry meetings were obviously the eyes and ears of the magistrates in making suitable appointments. Whilst not daring to instruct the Justice in his choice, the opinion and suggestions of the vestry committee would be sought and respected. Such was the case in Lamerton, where strong recommendations had been made for the disposition of "Two constables for the In Down and one for the Out Down". Tavistock parish vestry seems to have set a precedent in appointing professional and paid officers in their choice of Merritt, Physick and the like. It would surely be only a matter of time before their example would be followed...

The large parish of Bere Ferrers, with the greatest number of constables conscripted for duty, was naturally the first to follow this example. Constable William Mullard, in 1843, was receiving 24 shillings a week from the parish as the first full-time paid officer of the law in any of the rural parishes around the West Devon area. He remained in post for several years, although he did have to take a cut in pay some 7 years later, his increment being reduced by 4 shillings per week. Other parishes, like Lamerton, feeling that they ought to respect such change as being progress, were not, however, willing to pay a weekly salary; a £2 a year honorarium would satisfy the financial desires of their officers,

List of Persons Qualified and Liable, and duly Nominated by a Vestry, to Serve as Constables for the Parish of *Lamerton* in the Division of Tavistock, in the County of Devon, for the year 1852.

CHRISTIAN AND SURNAME.	PLACE OF ABODE.	TITLE, QUALITY, CALLING, OR BUSINESS.
John Percy	Lamerton	Registrar
William Brook	Whitslade	Yeoman
William Percy	Hardwell	Yeoman
Arthur Stanbury	Woolly	Yeoman
Samuel Palmer	Treveen	Yeoman
William Rice	North Brenton	Yeoman
William Cook	South Brenton	Blacksmith
John Williams	Woodmanswell	Yeoman
		Yeoman

NOTICE.—All objections to the foregoing List will be heard by Her Majesty's Justices of the Peace, acting for the said Division, at the Guildhall, in Tavistock, on *Tuesday* the —— day of *April* 1852, at *eleven* o'clock in the *fore* noon.

Overseers' Return of Constables.—Printed

R. CHAVE, Tavistock.

Overseers of the Poor of the Parish of *Lamerton*

instead. Other parishes soon followed, and Whitchurch and Milton Abbot fell into line, but the smaller parish of Sampford Spiney only gave the idea 12 months before resorting back to the old conscripted system of unpaid officials. However, Constables William Davey and John Wise, officers of that parish for quite some time, started receiving financial reward for their duties in 1846. Nevertheless, Wise clearly felt that his shoemaking business in the village was a far more lucrative proposition because he was to carry on his trade for many years to come. Whitchurch parish, likewise, felt that 10 shillings a week was sufficient payment for its constables when they increased their establishment from two to three officers. It was the likes of Mary Tavy parish that seemed to voice the opinion of many others in the West Devon area though, when, in 1843, they stated rather tersely "The parishioners deem it unnecessary to have any paid constables." Their attitude influenced the decisions of others for sure. They stuck to the old 'expenses only' payment system that had been in place for the many preceding years of the century.

Like their modern-day 20th century counterpart, this new breed of paid constables became objects of unfair attention. They were, after all, paid out of the pockets of the taxpayer, so an easy target. Many in the community felt that the salaried officer must defend himself in daring to receive wages for his duties. Many felt quite justified in placing strictures upon his life, both on and off duty. John Physick, Superintendent Merritt's deputy, soon fell foul of such unwarranted attention. In 1845 he was reprimanded by a meeting of the town's ratepayers for "failing in his duties". The rural constable, likewise, could expect no mercy once he was receiving wages. In the meantime, the residents of Bere Ferrers soon joined the local anti-police lobby when, on 22nd July 1845, a miner's wife, Mrs Mary Dennis, complained of Constable William Mullard. This, in turn, led to a report appearing in the *Tavistock Gazette* in which she alleged that he had "...while in a drunken state, assaulted her and beaten her". The magistrates, though, clearly felt that justice would not be done if they were to convict Mullard, and acquitted him. But it would be only the following year when Mullard was again subjected to unwarranted attention. On 23rd April 1846 three residents of the village placed allegations before the court claiming all sorts of offences committed by Mullard. One claimed that "he did incite and procure many persons, inhabitants of the said parish of Beer Ferrers, to enter a certain licensed beerhouse kept by Richard Jewell, for the purpose of tippling. And that the said William Mullard did continue in the same public house with the same persons, tippling at their expense. And whilst there, was guilty of using dissolute, profane, obscene, and disgusting language, and of other kinds of impropriety and misconduct". Another informant complained that during 1844 Mullard had indecently assaulted his wife. Why he had let this allegation lie low for 2 years before making it, is perhaps justification itself in suggesting that Mullard was now becoming unpopular in the village – as a "paid official of the law". Such is the tribulation of those in present times who choose to wear the uniform of the Sovereign in the name of the law.

A third allegation was placed before the court that day about the conduct of Constable Mullard. It suggested that he had known of card-playing going on in the premises of Richard Jewell's pub and that he "had been conniving at this outrage". What the court decided is unfortunately not recorded, but later that year further suggestions were made of Mullard. One can only surmise that the episode of the previous April had gone unproved, thus leaving the way open for another try to discredit him. This time it was John Goddard's allegation of assault by Mullard upon Mrs Goddard that went unproved by the Justices. Again, a few years later, it went unproved when Goddard alleged that Mullard had abducted his daughter. It was also said that he had hit Goddard's son over the head so hard that the lad had been left more or less insane ever since. In addition, Goddard had suggested that Mullard had been involved in fraudulent dealings with a mine company; it was this allegation, perhaps, that provided the straw to break the back of the patience of the judicial system because no further complaints are recorded against Mullard, who returned to duty in the parish, carrying on for many more years.

The complaints against Mullard seemed to have dried up, perhaps because the residents felt that there was little chance of rightful justice being meted out against an officer of the law, or perhaps because they realised that their scam of unwarranted and false accusations against their local constable would never succeed. We will never know. Unfortunately, in 1853, the paid constable of Milton Abbot, one John Wise, fell foul of the same suggestions and treatment by his parishioners. He must have questioned whether receiving a salary for his duties was such a good idea. Whatever, on April 5th that year, Robert Prout, a villager, alleged six offences against him, including making false arrests, receiving illegal payments, conducting improper interviews and lying about rate payment. Furthermore, that Wise falsely accused Prout of hiding in the village pub at 1.30 in the morning of Boxing Day! On top of all this, the offence to take the biscuit was "obscene exposure of your person to a woman". In the event, Wise survived it all, and Prout was subsequently charged with perjury, a warning to others who might follow the example of the likes of Goddard and Prout. These officers' cases proved beyond doubt that they were, then as they are now, most vulnerable to the suggestions of anyone wishing to bring them down. Even then it was realised that significant reforms should come about if the policing of the area was to be established and respected.

❋ ❋ ❋ ❋ ❋

Chapter 5

THE DEVON CONSTABULARY ARRIVES

(The county force takes over in Tavistock)

Tavistock police station c1885. Note the constable coming through the gate.

S. Lang

Reforms came wholesale in the November of 1856 when the Devon Constabulary was created. But it was not until the spring of 1857 that the newly formed county police force arrived in the West Devon area and the divisional boundaries were set up. Tavistock was selected as being placed sufficiently central in West Devon to warrant it being the divisional headquarters of the 'K' division; it was to remain as such for 70 years, until 1926. A superintendent was stationed in charge of the division, his office being in the guildhall, where his parish predecessor, Merritt, had been ensconced. The new superintendent was actually Mr Benjamin Hill and he had two sergeants – Sergeant Connell at Tavistock and Sergeant Cooksley at Lifton. There were eighteen constables in the division. Four were stationed in Tavistock town and the remainder were placed in cottages and houses rented in some of the villages around West Devon. These village outposts were at Bere Alston, Bere Ferrers, Bratton Clovelly, Bridestowe, Broadwoodwidger, Chillaton, Horrabridge, Lamerton, Lewdown, Lifton, Mary Tavy, Milton Abbot, Morwellham and Princetown – but not Yelverton as that area then came under the control of the Stonehouse division. The constables' pay of £1 a week was about in line with their parish-appointed forebears, but the sergeants received an extra 3 shillings a week. Like their predecessors, they were all subject to scrutiny and criticism at every corner, some justified and some otherwise.

One might surmise that the criticism levelled at the behaviour of the first of these new sergeants in Tavistock, Connell, fell into the category of being totally justified. In the September of 1857 he disrupted a public meeting, where the Hungarian nationalist leader named Kossuth was addressing an audience at The Bedford Hotel. The report in the *Tavistock Gazette* certainly pulled no punches when it stated "Soon after Kossuth commenced his lecture he met with frequent interruptions from some insolent intruder at the lower end of the room, and at last was obliged to stop. The obnoxious disturber was no less a personage than Connell, the Sergeant of Police, in a state of bestial intoxication. Is this a specimen of the men imposed by Lord Palmerston upon the nation at a costly expense? The only man at a public gathering of the people of a disorderly character was the person whose duty it was to maintain order. His conduct was so disgraceful as to justify his immediate removal. To the honour of our old police let it be said that for the many years of their office they never disgraced themselves as Connell did at Kossuth's lecture." The outcome was that Connell subsequently appeared before the magistrates and pleaded guilty to a charge of being drunk and disorderly. He was fined five shillings with seven shillings costs, and dismissed from the service. Unfortunately, in the same court, Constable Ireland was also dismissed "for some disgusting conduct at one of the public houses in the town".

The full and shocking details of exactly what Constable Ireland did are not recorded, but the fact remained that two of the new professional policemen had been dismissed for misconduct – already! The force would have to work much harder at convincing the reluctant public that they were a viable alternative to the locally appointed, unprofessional officers they had replaced. As if this was not enough, just 8 weeks later the following letter appeared in the *Tavistock Gazette*:–

"Sir, I was standing by my door in Higher Market Street with my two lodgers on the evening of Sunday week, when the newly appointed Sergeant of Police came up and said that we must be a pretty set of fellows to be up at that time (it was 11 o'clock) and, in an insolent manner, ordered us in. Now, Sir, I presume the ratepayers do not pay their money to support such men as these, and, if the new Police, instead of insulting respected tradesmen, and interfering with unoffending persons conversing in the street, were to endeavour to discover the authors of the late dastardly outrages on property in Tavistock, they would be more liked, and do more good."

By 1864 Superintendent William White Standfast Pickford was in charge, with a new sergeant, one Samuel Wellington, overseeing the constables in Tavistock. Perhaps the Constabulary felt that a change in command might encourage a change in fortune and opinion. If this was a conscious decision, it proved to be a wrong one for Captain William Henry Gardener Cornwall replaced Pickford within 11 years. His duties as the divisional superintendent were soon extended, like his predecessor, to include those of the inspector of both weights and measures and the diseases of animals. Small financial remuneration was received for these duties through the court, which at this time sat fortnightly on a Wednesday in the guildhall. The uniform dress at the time included a box-cap, later to be replaced by the pickelhaub in 1876. Not too dissimilar to the modern-day helmet, the Chief Constable entered into a 3-year contract for the supply of these at 9 shillings each. It was an item which the public called 'the new Prussian style helmets', but their opinions about the, 'revolutionary', new constabulary were not made any the healthier. A suggestion was made about this time by the Board of Guardians to the effect that the public health duties of the town ought to be passed to the police. This brought a positive refusal from the Chief Constable owing to the pressing and time-consuming duties that his officers had to undertake. The retort from one of the Board that "He had never yet seen an overworked policeman" must have created much hilarity in the town.

Superintendent Cornwall was soon to make his mark, and his surviving copy letters book(7) gives proof of his strict codes of discipline. The unfortunate constable at Princetown was soon to realise that the Devon Constabulary would not look lightly upon incivility, even if it was from a policeman's wife. When, on 7th May 1875, Superintendent Cornwall rode out and visited the remote station on the moors he found the quarters in "a very dirty state". The constable's wife had the audacity to question the superintendent's judgement. Despite her husband's efforts to quieten her and send her indoors, the family were removed to another station by the end of the week! The attitude of the superintendent was not always so draconian, though. For example, at the ceremony of the laying of the foundation stone of Kelly College in the town on 29th May that year, he secured private employment for many of his constables, thus providing an opportunity for them to supplement their meagre incomes. Perhaps the fact that Mr Kelly was a member of the police authority had some bearing on the matter but, whatever, Mr Cornwall could well be regarded as being far-sighted and ahead of his time. This is particularly so when one considers that private employment and sponsorship of officers by health authorities in hospitals in the latter years of the 20th century is thought of as a bold and progressively new idea.

The Chief Constable of the force at this time was Gerald de Courcy Hamilton. His order 858(2) of 27th March 1876 set out three pages of strictures relating to the required dress of officers and men of his force. Woe betide any officer whose turn out fell short of the required standards. An officer was issued with one uniform each year and was given the opportunity to purchase his previous year's uniform to use as second best. Many of the constables would, no doubt, have found it difficult to raise the half crown for a greatcoat or one shilling and fourpence for a tunic. As it was, policemen often resorted to other means to help out with family bills, and the force acknowledged their desire to keep livestock and fowls. An order(2) of November 1876 stated "A list of all members of the Force residing in station houses having permission to keep fowls etc. ... is to be sent to Headquarters with names, stations and by whom authorised". (One is left wondering at the fate of 'unauthorised fowls'!)

A sergeant and three constables in the Devon Constabulary uniform of 1869.
Devon & Cornwall Constabulary

Upon removal to another station, the force realised that their officers were in need of expenses, so granted ten pence for married men and three pence for single constables per mile. This was applied for, as the order goes on, "by way of a form number 10". More, modern-day, constables of a century later were still using forms 'number 10' for their removals – the wheels of progress move mighty slow sometimes!

Monthly pay parades, a tradition that was to last for a further 80 years in the Devon Constabulary, were held at divisional headquarters, the men from the villages having to march to their superintendent to receive their wages. The Chief Constable then ordered, in April of 1877(2), that "The new Uniform is to be fitted on the next Pay Parade. Should the weather be wet or look threatening the new clothing will not be worn on the march to the place of assembly, but must be carried and put on for the parade, it can be taken home by each constable, but will not be taken into wear until further orders." (No doubt the new uniforms would have been authorised by the time of the annual inspection of the Constabulary by Her Majesty's Inspector at Tavistock on 16th May that year).

The spirit of discipline and respect applied to the superintendent as much as it did the sergeants and constables of the time. When the superintendent felt it time to have a day off he was required to submit a request to the Chief Constable: Superintendent Cornwall's request of 2nd October 1877(7) was in typical style:-

"To The Chief Constable of Devon
Constabulary Barracks
Exeter
Sir
I have the honour to request that you will grant me leave of absence from October the 9th to the 18th inst. Both days being inclusive. I shall, however, return to Tavistock for the annual fair on October the 11th.
I remain, Sir, your obedient servant"

(It is encouraging to know that then, as now, no officer could ever contemplate getting 'Goose Fair Day' away from duty! At the same time it is interesting to note that at the date of the request – and up until being moved to Middlemoor on the outskirts of Exeter in 1939 – the headquarters of the Devon Constabulary was at 'Constabulary Barracks', Exeter, the building being adjacent to Exeter Prison. This building is now used as the prison administration offices).

Chapter 6

A POPULAR REFORMER

(Superintendent William Mitchell takes charge)

Superintendent William Mitchell of the Tavistock 'K' division, 1885.
Mrs Launa Mitchell

The fortunes of the Devon Constabulary were soon to take a turn for the better. On 29th June 1878, in his order(2) number 936, the Chief Constable, Gerald de Courcy Hamilton, instructed thus:-

"In accordance with the spirit of circular 953 the undermentioned exchange of Divisions between Superintendents will take place as soon as practicable:–

Superintendent Vaughan "F"	to	"A"
Superintendent Mitchell "A"	to	"K"
Superintendent Cornwall "K"	to	"F"

Signed G de Courcy Hamilton
Chief Constable of Devon.

It was on 16th August 1878 that the new superintendent, William Mitchell, wrote(7) to the Chief Constable as follows:–

"Sir,
I have the honour to report for your information that I removed from Barnstaple to Tavistock by first train yesterday, and this day Superintendent Cornwall has handed over the command of the K Division according to your orders.
I have the honour to be, Sir
Your obedient servant,
William Mitchell,
Sup't."

Superintendent Mitchell was to remain at Tavistock for 14 years. Without doubt, as his painstakingly, copper-plate written log books and records show, he was responsible for rejuvenating the public opinion about the Devon Constabulary that was so lacking in the area. His correspondence book(7) was inherited from Superintendent Cornwall and contains over 200 entries. It is an enlightening and graphic account of the history of the policing of the Tavistock and West Devon area for the last quarter of the 19th century.

Mitchell, as superintendent, along with one sergeant and three constables, was based in Tavistock. One sergeant and one constable were stationed at Lifton, and the remaining constables were distributed in the villages of Bratton Clovelly, Bere Alston, Beertown (Bere Ferrers), Bridestowe, Broadwoodwidger, Chillaton, Horrabridge, Milton Abbot, Morwellham, Lewdown, Lamerton, Mary Tavy and Princetown. Later, this establishment was increased by two officers, one at Whitchurch and the other at Lydford.

William Mitchell, as well as being a popular officer of the division, was also a devoted family man. He was supplied with accommodation at 'Rose Villa' in Butcher Park Hill, above the workhouse, and had a large family of four sons and three daughters. One of his sons, Arthur, went on to join the Metropolitan Police and was renowned as being amongst the officers to cross the Atlantic in 1910 to apprehend the murderer Crippen. Another son, Alfred, became a well-respected artist, exhibiting at the Royal Academy. A third son, Horace, emigrated to Canada to become a taxidermist, but was to meet up again some years later with

Arthur on his famous trip across the Atlantic.

Although being in charge of the division, Mitchell was, of course, answerable to the orders of the Chief Constable. Passing on the more unpopular orders from headquarters would surely have strained the patience of his men at Tavistock, despite their regard for him. For example, the Chief Constable's order(2) in February 1880 instructed that "The weather, having amended, and two serious Burglaries at Country Houses having occurred in one week, the seven hours night and three hours day duty will at once be resumed." In the following winter, however, the Chief Constable was to relent and permit the superintendents to use their discretion during the severe weather with respect to the night duty hours of the country beat constable. Doubtless, this was greeted somewhat more favourably!

The hours of duty worked by constables on their beats allowed for little time off. Attending church on Sunday was regarded as duty, and questions would be raised if an officer be caught out of uniform. A later instruction from headquarters in 1880 insisted that "in making out the new conference sheets care is to be taken to make every night conference at the houses of the nobility, gentry, clergy and principal ratepayers or at such buildings and places as would be likely to offer temptation to burglars." It was, after all, the 19th century and an age of inequality, with a great divide between the rich and poor.

Conference points were places on a beat where the constable had to make for at set times. Before the days of radios, the sergeant and superintendent needed to know where, at any set time, a constable would be on his beat. Thus conference points were set up and it was a serious disciplinary offence to fail to make a point without proper reason. The conference points of latter years were often made at telephone kiosks so that the sergeant could ring the constable at the given time.

By now Superintendent Mitchell's commitment to duty and, no doubt, sense of compassion, had already been tested. At Horrabridge railway station on the evening of 27th November 1878 he had been witness to a fatal accident on the line(7) – a Mr Martin, a guard on the London & South Western goods train, had been killed instantly. This accident had occurred on the Yelverton side of the Walkham river, so was outside the area of the Tavistock division, whose boundary at that time did not include the land on the Yelverton side of the Walkham. Nevertheless, Mitchell had directed Constable Jones at once to march to Stonehouse to inform the coroner and superintendent in charge of this, the 'H' division.

Mitchell, through his notes, clearly showed that he was constantly in search of a balance between compassion for his officers and commitment to his duty. His skill in this respect was regrettably often tested, especially in days when illness and death were more commonplace than the population would wish. His officers were no exception to the effects of illness. When 2nd Class Constable Howard of Bridestowe succumbed to bronchitis in the March of 1879, the superintendent ordered at once six local constables to act as bearers at his village funeral.

The effects of the loss of the Bridestowe constable on the parish were soon felt, for the navvies building the peat railway up to the Rattlebrook over the moors were a troublesome lot. Mitchell wrote urgently to the Chief Constable(7) "It will be necessary to fill this station immediately as there are a great number of navvies lodging at Bridestowe and Sourton, in consequence of the railway workings, at and near Bridestowe and a tram rail onto the moor. At night, sometimes, Bridestowe is very noisy." The following year he voiced concerns that Sergeant Cooksley at Lifton was very weak from a chest complaint and feared that another winter's duty might be too much for him. His regard for welfare did not stop at his men, but the population of Tavistock received attention from this compassionate man. It was he, in the November of 1881, that reported to the Chief Constable in answer to the order 1159(2) of that month "Sir, I have the honour to report that the Acts restraining the employment of children in sweeping chimneys are strictly complied with in this Division".

Mitchell's book provides details of constables' names and stations, misdemeanours and matters of discipline. When he came across situations where others might place men on charges, it was typical for him to display loyalty to his men, without seeming weak. His submission to the Chief Constable of 15th September 1882 suggests that: "I have the honour to submit the following removals for your consideration. Second Class Constable Yelland from Princetown to Mary Tavy, First Class Constable Vanstone from Lamerton to Princetown and Second Class Constable Chane from Tavistock to Lamerton."

Removals were not always as a result of matters of discipline. In the October of 1889 the building of the railways in the area caused Mitchell great consternation. The disorderly conduct of the navvies was a constant source of complaint. So much so that he temporarily closed Chillaton station and moved Constable Simpson to Bratton Clovelly in order that Constable Avent could be used to supplement the hard-pressed officer at Bere Alston. It seemed that the strategy worked for with two officers at Bere Alston for four months, the navvies were soon brought under control. He doesn't go on to say by what means or how many navvy's heads had to be stitched up, but the objective was achieved. He did, however, suggest in his request that Constable Avent was single, and very smart and strong!

William Mitchell retired from Tavistock, and was replaced, in the July of 1892, by a distinguished-looking Superintendent Richard Nicholls with his long white beard. Perhaps Nicholls might have had second thoughts about his new posting had he known what was in store for him – within a few months, a double murder occurred at Peter Tavy (this was indeed a baptism by fire for him). Meanwhile, the respect displayed for William Mitchell upon his retirement by his officers was suitably and eloquently demonstrated in the inscription on his presentation gift, a silver and crystal ink-stand. The inscription simply said:-

'Presented to
Mr W Mitchell
Late Superintendent of the K Division
as a small token of the respect by the Sergeants and Constables
on his retirement
July 1892'

No doubt there was insufficient room to describe exactly what form that respect took, but it is clear that a man of his calibre would be a hard act to follow with regard to commitment and compassion for the welfare of his men. He left the Tavistock area and returned to North Devon from whence he came, to end his days in the graveyard of the pretty church at Morthoe. As for his sons, Arthur retired as a detective inspector in the Metropolitan Police in 1925; Alfred became established as a well-known and regarded artist of his day (he was to return to the Tavistock area as an elderly bachelor before marrying a widow living at Double Waters, near Buckland, and carry on his painting until his death in 1948); and Horace and Wallace both settled and made new lives in Canada, as a taxidermist and a shipbuilder respectively. Sadly, one of his daughters – Aurelia – had died at Tavistock at the young age of 21, but as regards the other two, Elsie married and became a matron in Africa, while Bessy settled into married life with a small family.

And so ended a significant period in the policing of West Devon. William Mitchell left behind him a legacy of his correspondence book and an established structure of police houses in the villages which was to last a further 70 years with little change. The respect for the local police built up over those 14 years was a credit to him. He had arrived when things were very much different, but through his commitment and dedication left things for his replacement in a much-improved state. The policing of the area owed him much.

✳ ✳ ✳ ✳ ✳

Chapter 7

DIVISIONAL HEADQUARTERS

Tavistock. Divisional headquarters of the 'K' division from 1856 until 1921.

The guildhall had been the headquarters of the Tavistock Parish Police for 8 years since it opened in 1848. Now, in 1856, it was to play the same role for the 'K' division of the new Devon Constabulary, Tavistock having been identified as an excellent location from which to operate due to it being centrally placed in West Devon. It was decided that the senior officer for the division would be a superintendent and that he would travel about his area of responsibility on horseback. The horse, in turn, would be looked after by a constable for "not more than three hours a day" and could, when necessary, be tied to the ring that exists to this day by the front door of the police station.

The first senior officer was Superintendent Benjamin Hill, but he was to resign in the February of 1864 in order to take up a post as a stipendiary magistrate in Ireland. As a result, he was replaced a month later by William Standfast Pickford, whose duties included being the local inspector for the Contagious Diseases of Animals Act. This necessitated him travelling to enquire into breaches of the regulations, and it was on one such trip that his own horse caught glanders (a contagious horse disease) and had to be compulsorily slaughtered. The horse had been valued at £50, but the police authority were only disposed to allowing a grant of £20: his recent pay rise of twenty two pounds seven shillings and sixpence a year was taken up instantly in replacing his beast! With such hardships to endure, it was no surprise that Pickford resigned in the August of 1875.

Pickford was replaced within a fortnight by the newly appointed Superintendent William H. G. Cornwall. Although Cornwall only stayed until being removed to Torquay in the August of 1878, he certainly left his mark. His surviving correspondence book(7) portrays a disciplinarian and hard taskmaster. He was replaced by the popular Superintendent William Mitchell, an experienced divisional officer from Barnstaple with 14 years service in the rank already after having joined the Devon Constabulary only 3 years after its inception in 1856. His experience as an established divisional officer soon made its mark and he became a well-respected man. He also inherited Cornwall's correspondence book(7) and left a legacy of immense importance to police historians.

Mitchell was to retire in the July of 1892 and be replaced by Superintendent Richard Nicholls, a late starter in the promotion race. He had already been a policeman since 1857, having joined a few months after the formation of the Devon Constabulary, but it had not been until 1888 that he was promoted to superintendent – a surprising move after 31 years' service, because by then most men would have considered retirement. He eventually retired from Tavistock in the March of 1903, at the grand age of seventy-five!

The Chief Constable with senior officers, 1896. The white-bearded Superintendent Nicholls is on the right.

Devon & Cornwall Constabulary

Nicholls was succeeded by Captain William J. Gordon, a veteran of the great military campaigns of Queen Victoria's reign, a stickler for duty, but quick to praise when appropriate. It was in the May of 1910 that he wrote to Major Smalley of the 1st East Surrey Regiment, which was billeted with the local population, complimenting the troops on their behaviour. He was to remain in post as the superintendent of the 'K' division until its end in 1921. His last duty was to assemble the men of his division for a final photograph outside the court gate archway at the guildhall, a photograph which marked an unbroken 65 years as divisional headquarters of the 'K' division. He was then transferred to a new command and eventually retired in the February of 1936. In the meantime, with the 'K' division being disbanded, Tavistock and West Devon came under the command of the 'H' division at Crownhill.

The last of the Tavistock 'K' division, 1920:-

Back Row: PCs Hoare, Kellaway, Southwood, Loosemore, Freeman and Ash.
Middle Row: PCs Leach, Huxtable, Burridge, Sharp, Trump, Middlewick, West and Dymond.
Front Row: PC Moore, Sergeants Hill and Elworthy, Supt Gordon, Sergeant Snell, PCs Collins and Densham.

Author's collection

Crownhill. Divisional headquarters for Tavistock in the 'H' division from 1921 until 1945.

Divisional headquarters for Tavistock in the 'E' division from 1984 until 1994.

The old divisional headquarters at Stonehouse, near the port of Plymouth, was merged into the borough of Plymouth just prior to the Great War in 1914 and the old men of the Devon Constabulary at Stonehouse were 'lost' to the county force, along with the naval expression of the day "as big as a Stonehouse Policeman". This merger resulted in the divisional headquarters of the 'H' division being moved to Plympton for a few years until 1921, when the 'K' division at Tavistock was also disbanded. Thus Tavistock 'K' and Plympton 'H' divisions were amalgamated and came under the newly opened Crownhill station.

Superintendent Smith and Sergeant Jewell outside Crownhill police station, 1931.

Mrs J. Southgate

The 'H' division, with its new divisional headquarters, was divided up into sub-divisions, Tavistock retaining a little of its former status as a sub-divisional headquarters with an inspector in charge. Tavistock's policing area was again divided up into two sections, one based at Tavistock with a section sergeant and one at Lifton with its own sergeant. At the same time, the stations at Yelverton and Roborough came under the section sergeant at Crownhill, and so the situation remained through the turbulent years of the 1939 – 1945 war.

With increased mechanisation and vehicle ownership after the war, a new divisional 'wireless car' was introduced into the 'H' division and stationed at Roborough. It used the Plymouth City Police wavelengths and, by 1948, was proving its worth in catching stolen cars heading north out of the city into the county force area.

Then, as now, the city council sought to extend its boundaries. Under the Plymouth Extension Act of 1950, the village of Tamerton Foliot was 'lost' and taken under the administration of the city, although the Devon constable remained in the village. The special constables, meanwhile, refused to serve the city and remained in the County Constabulary. Perhaps credit should go to the little acknowledged efforts of the clerk to the Plympton Rural District Council, Percy Loosemore Esq. Mr Loosemore's father had been constable at Lamerton for many years and no doubt influenced his son's attitude towards a city take-over of the county area. And so Crownhill police station, divisional headquarters of the Devon County's 'H' division, became part of the Plymouth City Police jurisdiction: the 'H' division lost its headquarters and so retreated back to Plympton from where it had come in 1914. Crownhill and its distinctive Devon Constabulary police houses of 1929, just up the road towards Seaton Barracks, fell into the hands of the city force.

The Devon County Constabulary and the Plymouth City Police amalgamated in 1967, and so Crownhill came under the jurisdiction of Devon once again. But the old station, which once stood beside the Tamar public house in old Crownhill village, was one of a number of buildings demolished to make way for the new route of the A386 trunk road from the city northwards in the county, and few photographs remain of it. As a result, some wartime huts were taken over as the local police station. They, in turn, were vacated in the mid-1970s, when the fine, new Crownhill police station was built. Thereafter, the old huts served as a library until they, too, were demolished to make way for a car showroom.

Immediately upon being occupied, the new Crownhill station took over as the new divisional headquarters for the 'E' division of the Devon & Cornwall Constabulary. This was actually the old Plymouth City Police force area and resulted in the old city divisional headquarters (and city force headquarters) at Greenbank being closed. Of course, given these circumstances, it would be inevitable that the Plympton division would ultimately cease and, in 1984, this is exactly what happened: Crownhill took over and the Tavistock sub-division fell into the 'E' division until force reorganisation in 1994.

Plympton. Divisional headquarters for Tavistock in the 'H' division from 1950 until 1964.

Divisional headquarters for Tavistock in the 'G' division from 1966 until 1984.

With Stonehouse being taken into the Plymouth borough police area in 1914, the old Devon Constabulary 'H' divisional headquarters naturally went to Plympton. It was, after all, much bigger than the small village of Crownhill, itself some distance to the north of Plymouth. The 'H' division went as far north as the outpost at Yelverton.

Crownhill took command until the city force expanded in 1950, and again 'H' divisional headquarters retreated back to Plympton. The old men of the Plympton division remember it being affectionately known as the 'Happy H'. Perhaps the retreat from the city force encouraged a spirit of unity, but nothing other than contentment with their 'lot' is remembered. Later, in 1964, a reorganisation took place and Plympton division temporarily 'lost' the Tavistock sub-divisional area to Okehampton 'B' division in the north. However, this did not last long, for in 1966 Tavistock again returned to the Plympton division, then the divisional headquarters of 'G' division. The reorganisation of 1964 had also meant that Totnes, the former headquarters of the old 'G' division, was, itself, demoted and amalgamated into the Newton Abbot division. This left Plympton allocated the letter 'G' for its division. Meanwhile, the divisional radio room was situated at Plympton and remained so, sharing the Plymouth City radio waves until 1984, when the division ceased to exist.

The last bastion of the old Devon Constabulary surrendered to the Plymouth City some 16 years after the forces had amalgamated. Until then the 'E' division had occupied the old pre-1967 city force boundary. Even the men of the Devon & Cornwall Constabulary's 'E' division, who joined after the 1967 force amalgamations, were entrenched into the Plymouth City Police mould. Referring to the 'G' division officers as 'the county men', many of the pre-1967 officers of the old city force retained their city uniforms and ornately distinguished helmets.

If the 1967 amalgamation had been difficult to accept for the men of the old forces, the divisional boundary changes of 1984 confirmed that the 20th century had at last arrived. Tavistock lost its sub-divisional status, and Plympton became a sub-divisional headquarters under the new 'E' Plymouth division. The sub-divisional Chief Inspector at Tavistock, Ron Warren, removed to Cornwall, and was promoted to take

The Chief Constable with 'G' division senior officers, 1980.
Ch/Supt R. Studden, Mrs Joan Martin, Mr Bill Martin (Town Clerk of Tavistock), Ch/Insp Ron Warren, Mrs Anne Sherrell (Mayoress), Mr Ted Sherrell (Mayor of Tavistock), the Chief Constable, John Alderson, Supt L. Salter and Insp Derek Roper.

Ret'd Supt D. Roper

charge of the East Cornwall traffic area, while Chief Superintendent Studden, divisional commander of the old 'G' division, retired. At the same time Tavistock settled into its new role as a section station with an inspector – Derek Roper, at one time a constable at the Princetown beat.

Okehampton. Divisional headquarters for Tavistock from 1964 to 1966.

With the force reorganisation of 1964, Okehampton 'B' division took over Tavistock for a two-year period until 1966. But it was soon recognised that the influences upon Tavistock from Plymouth in the south were too great to be ignored and Tavistock again returned to Plympton, by now the headquarters for the 'G' division.

Totnes. Divisional headquarters for Tavistock in the 'J' division from 1994.

Massive changes forcewide came about in the mid-1990s when divisional boundaries came into line with local authority administrative boundaries. Tavistock, being in West Devon, came out of the Plymouth 'E' division, which assumed the Plymouth City Council boundary. It also led to the Dartmoor and South Hams 'J' division being formed, with its divisional headquarters based at Totnes taking in the whole of the West Devon, South Hams and Teignbridge Council areas, thereby accounting for 40% of the whole of the Devon county area.

Tavistock, as a sectional station, retained its inspector, but the chain of command had several links removed and, for the first time since 1921, answered directly to the divisional commander without the intermediary step through a sub-division. But the radio system and communications remained based at Plymouth, as they had done, with little interruption, since 1948. The influence of the Plymouth city and its travelling offender could not be overlooked, even by 'the county men'!

Force headquarters, Exeter.

Throughout this time of divisional changes one thing remained constant, the force headquarters of the old Devon and new Devon & Cornwall Constabularies always stayed at Exeter, in various homes admittedly. However, the overall command of the force remained in the hands of the various Chief Constables at Exeter, and looks like remaining so for the foreseeable future.

✳ ✳ ✳ ✳ ✳

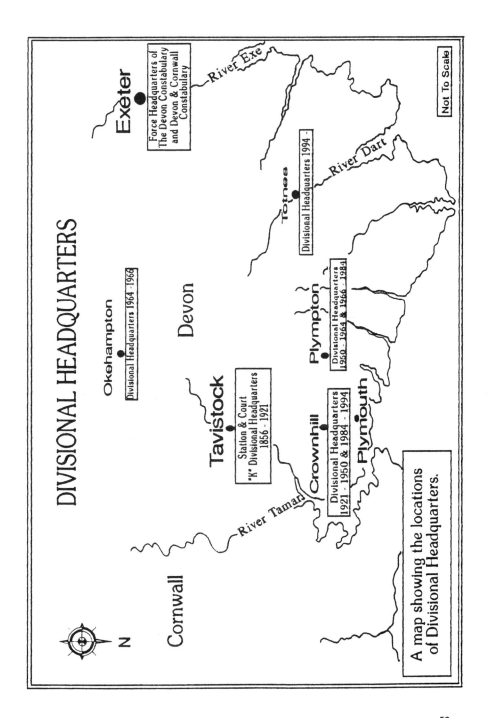

DIVISIONAL HEADQUARTERS

Exeter
Force Headquarters of The Devon Constabulary and Devon & Cornwall Constabulary

River Exe

River Dart

Totnes
Divisional Headquarters 1994 -

Okehampton
Divisional Headquarters 1964 - 1966

Devon

Plympton
Divisional Headquarters 1950 - 1964 & 1966 - 1984

Tavistock
Station & Court "K" Divisional Headquarters 1856 - 1921

Crownhill
Divisional Headquarters 1921 - 1950 & 1984 - 1994

Plymouth

River Tamar

Cornwall

N

Not To Scale

A map showing the locations of Divisional Headquarters.

Chapter 8

THE TAVISTOCK SECTION

Tavistock Station.

Despite the fact that, initially, Tavistock station was the divisional headquarters for the West Devon 'K' division, it only housed the three Devon constables for the town, and their sergeant, although the divisional superintendent did have his office in the building. Nowadays, though, the police station is 'home' to an inspector, three sergeants and fifteen constables. To supplement these officers there is the criminal investigation department, comprising a detective sergeant and two detective constables. The lone traffic warden also works out from the town's station, along with the three enquiry clerks. It was not always such. For many years after the Devon Constabulary took over the building in the mid-19th century, the station sergeant supervised just two constables. The present-day establishment has come about through the closure of country beat stations and the transfer of those officers into Tavistock station. The compliment of three sergeants is comprised of the original station sergeant, along with the two from both Yelverton and Lifton stations.

The policing of the 19th century Tavistock was a far cry from today's modern service. The attitude of the public to the police was very different, and within the service discipline was austere. The original station was below the court and had seven cells, or bridewells as they were called. They provided a rather imposing dungeon – so much so that on one night of January 1864 a German prisoner committed suicide in one cell. The newspaper of the day reported "A German, Matthias Ziscoven, aged about forty-five, locked up for begging, hung himself by his handkerchief to the hook of the cell door in Tavistock lock-up. On Monday night about one hour before midnight, the body, unattended by funeral rites, was carried to the grave. A large number of persons, principally young, witnessed the gloomy scene, many of whom showed in their behaviour while marching to the grave, an utter inability to realise the terrible solemnity of the occasion." Ziscoven's resting place was in Dolvin Road cemetery, in an unmarked grave.

An equally unfortunate death was that of a retired sergeant of police in the town. Sergeant 230 George Eveleigh had lived in the police house adjoining the station whilst he was at Tavistock from 1895 until 1902. He died in 1909 of tetanus brought about by stepping onto a rusty nail. Sergeant Eveleigh had served with Constable Bleakley Burrough, who resided in one of the two small cottages at the rear of the station. These two cottages, incidentally, had been built for the two constables at around the same time as Market Road and the diverting of the River Tavy. Moreover, they were to remain as police houses until the construction of Drake Villas, near Drake's statue, in the 1950s, when two of the new houses were taken into use by the police authority and the cottages became the police social club and the probation service office.

Sergeant George Eveleigh of Tavistock, 1895.

Mrs E. Hooper

Constable Bleakely Burrough of Tavistock, 1890.

Mrs J. Stewart

The superintendent's letter book(7) provides a wonderful record of policing matters of the day. Some routine incidents are detailed, but some are more significant to the running of the station. One of the more notable events was the great flood of 17th July 1890. The River Tavy burst its banks and flooded the station to a considerable depth. A prisoner had to be rescued from the cells and the dwellings of the constables and sergeant had to be evacuated. The cells were rendered uninhabitable and were condemned. Superintendent Mitchell wrote(7) quickly to the Chief Constable:–

"Sir

I have the honour to inform you that considerable damage has been done to the Tavistock Police Station by the flood this morning. The water was five feet high in my office and in the cells and quarters. A prisoner had to be brought out of the cells before the water rose. The Sergeant and constables had barely time to save their children. Some of the office books and nearly all the papers are rendered useless.

I have the honour to be

Sir

Your obedient Servant

William Mitchell

Supt."

As a direct result of the floods, the cells had to be replaced. New ones were started at once, but all prisoners had to be lodged at either Lifton or Stonehouse stations for the two years of construction work. The new cells were then opened in 1892, and are still in use to this day for the same purpose. They have in their time lodged some interesting subjects, including a German aircraft crew shot down during the last war: their aircraft narrowly missed Bannawell Street viaduct and crashed near Hurdwick Farm.

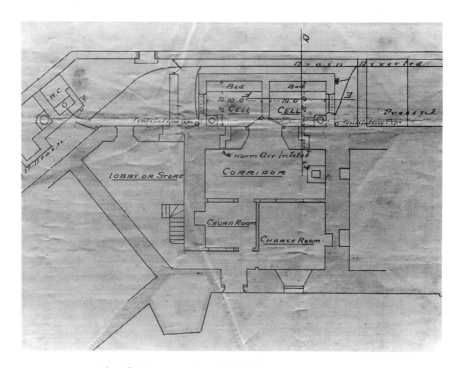

Plans for the new police cells, 1892.
Courtesy of Tavistock Museum

Once Tavistock ceased being a divisional headquarters, the superintendent was replaced by an inspector. The inspector took command of the Tavistock sub-division and, in effect, carried out the same duties as his predecessor, the superintendent. He lived, initially, at 6 Bedford Place (now demolished) on the site of the present Crown Leisure Centre. A new dwelling for the inspector was built at Crelake and is found just behind Crelake Stores in Whitchurch Road. One such inspector to occupy it was Frank Barnicoat, who had been a sergeant at

Sergeant Gale in his police cottage doorway, 1930.
Author's collection

Tavistock. He had been promoted whilst still on the station, something of a rarity in the day, and rose to the rank of superintendent before retiring in the 1950s. Many other inspectors have graced Tavistock over the years, including Paddy Bretell. He had been a constable in the 1930s at Yelverton and was subsequently stationed at Mary Tavy as the village officer. He returned to Tavistock some years later in the 1950s as inspector. Many of the retired men of Tavistock fondly remember him as a great snuff taker, whose dark uniform usually bore the evidence of his habit! He was to end his time in Tavistock running a guest house in Plymouth Road. Another, somewhat tall, inspector had been 'Tiny' Turner, as he was affectionately known. It was his grandson, Mark, who later became headmaster of Kelly College in the town.

'H' division, September 1958:—

Back Row: MPC Ivor Foster (Tavistock Motor Patrol), PC Ken Tonkins (Bratton Clovelly), PC Gordon Hellyer (Tavistock), PC Peter Nelson (Lewdown), PC ?, PC Bill Ridgeway (Roborough), MPC Ivor Neale (Plympton Motor Patrol), DC Bob Forrow (Plympton CID), MPC John Bickley (Plympton Motor Patrol), PC Tom Slater (Ivybridge), PC Harry Willcocks (Cornwood), PC Ian Wright (Plympton), PC Eddie Willey (Station unknown), PC Mike Nelson (Plympton), PC Max Faulkener (Horrabridge), DC Jack Harris (Plympton CID).

Middle Row: PC Keith Priddis (Plympton), DC "Ozzie" Osbourne (Plympton CID), PC Charlie Parsons (Plympton), PC Arthur Stephens (Station unknown), PC Bill Lobb (Tavistock), PC Louis Woodgates (Tavistock Motor Patrol), PC Peter Dunnsford (Elburton), PC Tony Avery (Yelverton), PC George Rollings (Plympton), PC John Holman (Plympton), PC Pat Docherty (Staddiscombe), PC ?, PC Ted Clifford (Plympton), PC Bill Badcock (Milton Abbot), Cadet Tony Berry (Plympton), PC Fred Chapel (Plympton), DC Tom Langman (Plympton CID), DC Peter Dobson (Plympton CID).

Front Row: Typist Mary Getheridge (Plympton), Sgt Hawkins (Plympton Motor Patrol), Sgt Jack Street (South Brent), Sgt Sid Matthews (Plympton), D/Sgt Jack Tarr (Plympton CID), Sgt Len Doble (Oreston), Insp Paddy Bretell (Tavistock), Supt Bert Roper (Plympton), Insp Sid Badcock (Plympton), Sgt ?, Sgt Alfred Fayter (Plympton), Sgt Len Clode (Lifton), Sgt/Clerk unknown name (Plympton), Typist Vi Woods (Plympton).

Ret'd Constable Mike Nelson

Mrs G. Lugg

Plympton 'H' division, 1941.–

Included in the photograph are Inspector Wiltshire of Tavistock (front row – eighth from left), Sergeant Burrows of Yelverton (front row – fourth from left) and Sergeant Perryman of Lifton (front row – fifth from left).

The inspectors at Tavistock all took a great pride in the station and 'their' town, many being seen on the streets in the evening as much as their young constables. On one such night a prisoner had escaped from Dartmoor Prison. The inspector was informed that the escapee had been sighted in the town, and so decided to accompany the sergeant in making a search of the alleyways and lanes. Whilst checking an alley in Brook Street he attempted to open a doorway, but found it being held shut. So he put his full weight against it and broke it off its hinges. The door then collapsed inwards on top of a heap of rubbish. A check was made of the alley to no avail, but when the door was lifted up the heap of rubbish was found to be none other than an unconscious escaped prisoner!

During the war years of the 1940s Inspector Wiltshire was stationed at Tavistock, followed by Inspector Derges. Inspector Derges had been sergeant at Lifton some years before. Other inspectors included Newman, Luscombe and Reid.

Inspector Newman looks on as Princess Elizabeth is introduced to the Town Band, c1949.
Courtesy of Tavistock Times Gazette

In later years, as a sub-divisional headquarters, Tavistock boasted a Chief Inspector as well as an inspector. Chief Inspector Ron Warren was for a few years, in the early 1980s, stationed as the police chief for the area. His deputy was Inspector Derek Roper, once a constable at Princetown. When Chief Inspector Warren left, Inspector Roper took command. He, in turn, was succeeded by Inspector Peter Ayres, who

Above: Inspector Ken Reid of Tavistock, 1966 (in Devon
Constabulary uniform).

Jim Thorrington

Below: Inspector Peter Ayres of Tavistock, 1985.

Jim Thorrington/P. Ayres

had been promoted on station from sergeant. In fact, he had been at Tavistock most of his service, having held the ranks of constable, detective constable and sergeant in the town before becoming inspector. When he retired other officers followed him, including John Hatch and Mark Chown. The present inspector, Colin Draper, had been sergeant at the station in the early part of the 1980s.

The sergeant's quarters were vacated by the early 1970s, after the Courtlands Road police houses had been built. In its time, however, the police cottage was host to a number of officers destined for higher places. These included Rupert Hardwell, who went on to become the divisional commander for the Plympton division in the early 1960s, and Sergeant Derek Fowkes, who later became superintendent at Barnstaple. Another occupant was Sergeant Brian Phillips, who had been stationed in the late 1950s as a young constable at Yelverton. He was destined, ultimately, to retire as Assistant Chief Constable of the force.

Sergeant Brian Phillips and Constable Pat Gibson of Tavistock, 1965.
B. Phillips/Ian Wooldridge, Devon & Cornwall News & Picture Agency

Sergeant Bob Thomas and Constable Ken Northey of Tavistock, 1949.

K. Northey

Some sergeants, however, remained as they were. Sergeant Bob Thomas, who lived in the cottage in the post-war years, was a well-liked officer. His cottage was shared by the station single man, Constable Ken Northey. Ken later became constable at Lydford, then moved on to the traffic division and was stationed at Tavistock motor patrol in the late 1950s. A spare bedroom, now used as the C.I.D. office, provided accommodation for the third constable stationed in the town. Constable Ken Northey resided in that spare room in the late 1940s, sharing the sergeant's bathroom. Sergeant Thomas is rarely remembered being out of uniform, such was the commitment to duty of the officers of the day.

The single quarters were not, however, always in the sergeant's house. In later years the attic rooms above the magistrates court provided bedrooms for two young, unmarried constables. Constable Dick Norrish, later to be stationed at Lewdown, was the last of the single men at the station. Their meals were taken out in a local guest house. Later, though, their bedrooms were converted into the station kitchen and meal room. It was Sergeant Fowkes who commandeered the extra single man's bedroom for use as part of the sergeants' cottage. He had a large family and needed the extra bedroom, which never returned to its former use to house an unmarried constable.

The last of the sergeants to live in the cottage was Sergeant Dennis Connell. It had then been taken over by the social services department for use as offices, and the town's sergeant movd up to the Courtlands Road houses. As the rural stations closed so their sergeants were also moved to the Courtlands Road houses in Tavistock, to join in with a shift pattern. Sergeant John Bickley, who had been the last sergeant at Yelverton, was one such officer. He remained for some years at Tavistock until moving away to Launceston; he did, however, come back as enquiry clerk until his retirement in the early 1990s. His two sons, both sergeants themselves, paid a surprise visit to the station on his last day to wish him a happy retirement!

John Bickley photographed with sons, Stephen and Andrew, on his last day, 1995.

Jim Thorrington

To list the constables who have been stationed at Tavistock over the years would be an impossibility, even though up until the late 1950s a book was kept of officers who had served in the area. In fact, Constable Jack Lamacraft had been particularly keen on recording the names of officers in his book, but alas it is now gone.

The shift system, like many aspects of policing, is now very different. For much of the time constables worked a split shift system. Their day's duty was split inconveniently into two parts and followed these general hours:–

Earlies	6am – 10am	then	2pm – 6pm
Days	8am – noon	then	4pm – 8pm
Days	9am – 1pm	then	2pm – 6pm
Lates	1pm – 5pm	then	7pm – 11pm
Nights	2pm – 6pm	then	10pm – 2am

It was not until 1957 that the split shift system was abolished, to the general delight of all, being replaced by an eight-hour shift, usually comprising:–

Earlies	6am – 2pm
Lates	2pm – 10pm
Nights	10pm – 6am

If the sergeant was away for any reason the senior constable would take his place and become acting sergeant. Sometimes the senior man was one of the rural beat men from the police houses in the surrounding villages of West Devon.

Constable Dick Hancock of Tavistock, 1975.
Mrs H. Hancock

Constable Hancock inspects shotgun damage to his police car, 1976.

Mrs H. Hancock

It was not until the closure of all but a few of these stations that the modern-day community constable position was created. Designed to replace the gap left by the village constables, the Chief Constable of the day, John Alderson, developed a policing system still used in most stations: constables were allocated designated areas for responsibility whilst still being able to speedily respond to emergencies. These were the new community constables, created in the mid-1970s.

Tavistock's first community policeman was Constable Dick Hancock. He had been stationed at Tavistock for as long as anyone could recall! Consequently, he was a natural choice for the job on his cycle. Dick had originally come to Tavistock as a motor patrol officer in the Devon Constabulary days, but remained at the town when the traffic department moved to Okehampton. In his time at Tavistock he was involved in a number of incidents, including having his 'panda car' shot at when a local gun dealer's shop was ransacked. He was, in turn, replaced by others – Derek Roberts, Trevor Masters and Diane Worth.

Above: Constable Trevor Masters of Tavistock, 1980.
Tavistock Times/Jim Thorrington

Below: The author with his wife, Shirley, and children, Matthew and Laura, collecting his M.B.E. at Buckingham Palace, February 1997.

Courtesy of Charles Green Photography

Then, in 1985, the author of this book became the town's community constable after being one of the patrol officers for some years in the town. He was to remain in post for a further 11 years as the community officer, not leaving until 1996, and a few months later he was mentioned in the New Year's Honours, being appointed an M.B.E. for his services to the community.

Returning now to earlier times, a new problem that arose was that associated with the coming of the motor car – traffic congestion. Soon police officers were being used more and more to stand on busy points on main roads in order to direct traffic and relieve congestion, and by the 1930s it was realised that these officers were not being used very well. As a result, a new branch of the police service soon developed, which led to the creation of the traffic warden. These officers, however, were not in the style of the modern-day warden, for there were no parking restrictions to enforce in such times. Instead, they were employed to stand on points and direct traffic.

At Crownhill, near Plymouth, there was a busy junction with the road heading, from the city, north to Tavistock on the A38, and the warden at the crossroads was Harold Southcott. He started work there in about 1932 and remained on that point until being transferred to Tavistock at the outbreak of World War II. Thereafter, he remained in Bedford Square for many years in his familiar white coat coping with the heavy traffic

Traffic Warden Harold Southcott in Bedford Square, Tavistock, c1940.

R. J. Allen

going through the town in the days when Tavistock was a major through route for Cornwall, Newbridge (at Gunnislake) being, at that time, the most southerly Tamar crossing for traffic without using the ferries. Indeed, he became quite a celebrity and tourist attraction until his retirement, but unfortunately few photographs of him at his point exist.

Mr Southcott was not replaced, and by 1962 the Tamar Bridge was open, thereby easing the traffic congestion somewhat. Nevertheless, Special Constable Frank Turner carried on this traffic duty point for quite some years on busy Saturdays and market days until (and after) the arrival of Tavistock's first true traffic warden, Mr 'Jim' Hext, complete

Traffic Warden Jim Hext's first day, 1965.

Tavistock Times

with yellow band. This was in the summer of 1965, and such a novelty attracted attention in the form of an article in the local *Tavistock Times* newspaper. Be that as it may, he remained patrolling the streets of the town for almost 15 years, when he left the uniform behind and went to work inside the police station as an enquiry office clerk dealing with telephone calls and routine enquiries from the public. His replacement, meanwhile, was Traffic Warden 'Toby' Croft. 'Toby' had been an evacuee from Plymouth to the town, as a boy, during the war years, and was a familiar face before he ever took on the role as warden on the streets. He remained for over 10 years until ill health forced an early retirement, and, in turn, was replaced – by the first lady warden, Carol

Above: Traffic Warden Toby Croft at Vigo Bridge, 1981.
Jim Thorrington

Below: Traffic Warden Carol Atkinson in Brook Street, 1996.
Mrs C. Atkinson

Atkinson. She had been a warden in Plymouth city but moved out to Tavistock when 'Toby' retired. For a short time, during the busy summer months, she was joined by a second warden – Lyn Bunyan – but finance and cuts could not support a second warden for long. Despite losing a finger to a stray dog some years ago, Carol's familiar good humour on the street reflects that traffic wardens really are human too!

Traditionally, the duty of providing a presence at the police station fell to the senior constable in the section. Having probably served over 25 years, walking the beat in all weathers, the comfort of working indoors and out of the elements was regarded as a privilege of service. Constables Bedford, Marsh and Connett are amongst some of the senior men to have held this position. The resident sergeant who occupied the cottage next to the station at Tavistock also provided support when required. Indeed, Sergeant Thomas (of Tavistock in the late 1940s) was rarely seen out of uniform, preferring instead to serve his vocation in the true spirit of a dedicated officer. The first enquiry office for the public to bring their problems to was situated under the steps leading up to the court front door. A rather small opening in a wall was provided, but this soon progressed into a more accessible position. The door at the foot of the station steps (until the early 1970s) provided the main front door for public access for over 100 years. With its familiar 'Devon Constabulary' arched sign above, this door was rarely shut before midnight.

It was not until the 1950s and 1960s that non-uniformed police staff were employed to work at the enquiry desk. One of the first of these able-bodied enquiry clerks was George Marsh, who provided a friendly face for the nervous visitor to the police station. His presence released constables to return to outside duties, no doubt to the dismay of the more senior ones! A telephone was installed in the police station at an early stage and 'Tavistock 17' was all the members of the public had to dial. The service provided to the public was improved by employing more clerks, and eventually the enquiry office was opened from 8am to midnight, seven days a week. This was labour intensive, and Mr Marsh was eventually joined by Douglas Jarrett and Jim Lloyd. The retiring traffic warden, 'Jim' Hext, also came into the office to service the public after some years out on the streets.

As time marched on and these clerks retired, they were replaced. Trevor Searle, a former officer in the Special Constabulary, joined the station along with Mrs Pat Roke, who had served as a typist at the station for many years after her time on the clerical staff at Dartmoor Prison. Eventually, one of the longest serving employees of the force – John Bickley – joined the staff as an enquiry clerk. He had served in the Devon Constabulary before amalgamation and retired as a sergeant, having served as the last in that rank at the Yelverton station. Geoff Jackman, a communications radio operator at Launceston, also moved to Tavistock when the East Cornwall control room at Launceston closed, and eventually the whole service was reviewed. The enquiry office now remains open ten hours a day, with an emergency telephone outside in the event of an urgent call being necessary in the early hours.

The enquiry office eventually moved from the lower part of the station to its present-day location in the late 1970s. The former sergeant's house, which had been used by social services in the town, was vacated when the new social services buildings were opened. The police station expanded sideways and the old sergeant's dining room and lounge now provide an office which bears no resemblance to their former use. The office is equipped with the very latest of technology: communications and computers are now the order of the day in the modern and busy police service. The old constables of the Devon Constabulary, keen to stay in out of the rain, would not recognise either the office or the service it now provides. Perhaps given the choice, walking around in the rainy lanes of Devon of 50 years ago might seem a rather more idyllic life after all!

For some years the Tavistock sub-division was home to a dog section, with Constables Bill Wedge and Paul Broad being the handlers, to name but a few. Their role took them all over the area, but they were here

Sergeant Brian Phillips and Constable Paul Broad, 1966.

B. Phillips

predominantly because of the prison. The nearest 'Devon' dogs were at Torquay, so they were in themselves an outpost of their department. Their two houses and kennels were situated in Whitchurch, near Crelake, but eventually, after the 1967 amalgamation with the Plymouth force, the dog section moved into the city.

No record of Tavistock police station could ever be complete without a mention of one of the greatest supporters of the local police, that being Mr Jim Thorrington and his wife Shirley. They reside in the small cottage adjoining the police station and are as much a part of the 'police family' as its officers. Having lived in the cottage for decades, Jim has been well known to all contemporary officers passing through the station as a great friend. Working as a photographer for the local press,

Jim and Shirley Thorrington, 1995.
J. Bird/Tavistock Times Gazette

he often accompanied the constables of the area to scenes of accidents and incidents to capture photographic evidence.

For want of space in such a small volume many names have had to be left from these pages. Their contribution, however, to the story and history of the policing of Tavistock is no less significant because of it. It is upon their duties and efforts that the modern-day service was born. The stories passed down from constable to constable do sometimes take some swallowing, but in the best traditions of service, practical jokes on a colleague were an essential part of the policeman's day. Perhaps in a modern service, demands and commitments are greater than ever before. Time for such humour is often short but, hopefully, a smile is not too difficult to find on the face of a 'Tavistock' policeman.

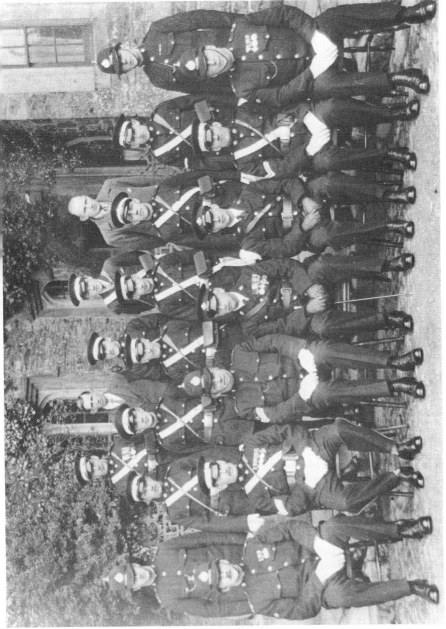

St John Ambulance Brigade and Tavistock policemen, 1930.
Tavistock Times Gazette

Bere Alston.

Bere Alston had proved to be a real challenge to the local police well before the days of the Devon Constabulary. It was therefore decided that in the first instance, the village deserved two officers living in the community. It was Constables Gist and Whimple that shared the responsibilities for quite some years between them. They were to be involved in a variety of incidents, not least of which was political unrest. At the times of forthcoming elections in the late 19th century, a local public house in Bere Alston used one of its rooms as a committee room for the Conservative Party. As one would expect this would not be to everyone's liking, and subsequently several windows of the pub were broken. Constables Gist and Whimple made enquiries but failed to identify the culprits. The two officers were also subject of concern by local residents in respect to disorder being committed at the Passage Inn, situated on the banks of the Tamar opposite Calstock. Steamer parties visited the inn from Plymouth, and subsequently drunkenness and disorder was reported. The superintendent, in replying to concerns expressed about the lack of police attention, explained that Constable Whimple suffered from heart disease and was not fit enough to fight the drunks, so it was left to the fitter Constable Gist to sort them out. The inn, he reported, is 3 miles from the station but the constable has a point there, so it had ample police attention.

The Bere Alston area suffered greatly in the October of 1889 when the railway was being built. Navvies living in the area caused the constables immense problems and, as a result, the Chillaton station was temporarily closed and an extra officer, Constable Avent, was drafted in from Bratton Clovelly for four months to help out. Once the railway was finished things quietened down and, eventually, the extra officer was restored back to his station. Bere Alston also lost its second constable and carried on with just the one.

By the start of the 20th century the police house at Bere Alston was situated at 14 Gallows Street, now known as Bedford Street. The name Gallows Street came from the fact that the gallows of the area used to stand at the top of the street on the outskirts of the village. The last constable living in this house was Constable Soper, and the evidence of the Soper family is still to be seen by the carving on the outside window sill. Young William Soper, the son of the constable, carved 'W.S.' in the sill without his father knowing prior to them leaving the village. Young William eventually admitted to the crime many years later, but fortunately he was aged over ninety when this information came into the hands of the police during the research of this book. Consequently, he was saved by the limitation of proceedings rules!

The police station for the village then moved to Tapp Hill, just down the road from Bedford Street. Other constables stationed at the village

Bere Alston police house – Gallows Street, 1911.

Mrs M. Taylor, Bere Ferrers Parish Council Clerk

included Constables Dymond and Trigger. Constable Trigger had formerly been stationed at Milton Abbot, and he eventually moved from Bere Alston to Mary Tavy. Constable Richards followed Trigger, and later Horace Benjafield arrived at the beat. When he retired he became an advisor to the 'Dixon of Dock Green' writers and producers. Benjafield was a methodical man for, when he was replaced in 1943 by Constable 93 Wilfred Jane, he left him a concise list of people on his beat. The list proved invaluable to the new constable in the area as it was a thumbnail sketch of characters who could be trusted and those who couldn't. A list of who to ask when in need and whom not to tell a word! Constable Jane was no newcomer to West Devon, however. He had been stationed at Princetown from 1934 until 1936, then taken over the Milton Abbot beat for three years before being moved to Tavistock from 1939 until 1943.

Constable Jane stayed at Bere Alston for 11 years until the mid-1950s, when he was moved (again) back to Tavistock as the senior constable. He was the last officer to occupy the Tapp Hill house, and the station eventually moved to the new, purpose-built police house on the Drake's Park estate nearby, now situated next to the fire station. The old station in Tapp Hill had a rear yard, and one resident constable once kept fowls there. Unfortunately, the local farmer, who the constable used to scrounge corn from, got slightly fed up with the constant requests for free corn and so decided to play a joke on the officer. As usual, the constable arrived at the farm with his cycle and left with a bag of corn over the handlebars. However, he did not notice in the darkness that the farmer had cut a small hole in the corner of the sack, and the result was that the constable left a trail of corn all the way from the farm to the back yard of the police house. The constable found another source for chicken feed after that!

It was not unknown for the older rural policemen of the day to arrive home with 'little gifts' from their beat. One local officer was the scourge of a farmer when, on night shift, he would nip over the hedge for a few cabbages. The farmer got wise to the times of the officer's night shift and lay in wait for him. When the constable had paid his visit to the cabbage field, he returned to his cycle in the hedge – only to find a bag full of cabbages hooked over the handlebars with a note saying "You only have to ask constable" attached thereto. The farmer didn't lose any more cabbages after that!

The old Tapp Hill house was sold and eventually bought by a local special constable. The front door of the old station was unceremoniously blocked up and a gas meter box fixed to the opening. It was the new police house at Drake's Park, though, that became the station that most residents of the village would remember. One new officer at the village in the mid-1960s was Constable John Hurn. He had been stationed at the Mary Tavy beat at the time when the Lydford station closed and was subsequently taken over by the Mary Tavy officer. This constable was required to ride a motorcycle, which John refused to do. He therefore swapped, quite happily, with Constable Roger Catterall of Bere Alston, who was keen to have a motorcycle instead of his bike. John was then quite content and remained for a few years until being replaced.

The last officer stationed in the village was Constable 292 Robert Cotton, who inherited the beat (but not pedal cycle!) from the much taller John Hurn. A keen sportsman, he featured in many of the police sports teams and remained in the village until the fateful day arrived in 1971 when Bere Alston said goodbye to their constable, who left for Salcombe station. After that Constable Cotton went on to greater things (as well as being the author's sergeant at one time at Falmouth in the 1970s!) and he retired at Barnstaple as a superintendent.

The village from that day came under the new 'panda car' scheme as seen on the popular 'Z Cars' television series of the day, operating out of Tavistock. The village retains an officer dedicated for its responsibility, the last of the long term ones being Constable Colin Passmore, who covered the area by motorcycle from Tavistock. The closure of the Bere Alston station, meanwhile, caused great consternation for one officer because it was none other than Wilfred Jane's son, Norman, who, as an inspector in the 'research and development department' at police headquarters, had to put the case together to prove the need for closure. Furthermore, at a presentation in the village Norman's supervisor could not attend and so he was left to carry the can! The village where he had grown up as a boy might have been a little unkind to their local man at his turning the tables on them, but this, fortunately, did not happen and

Constable Robert Cotton's last day at Bere Alston, 1971.

he returned to the village to spend his retirement years amongst friends and relations. Perhaps they realised that it was not his idea, and that he was just following unquestionable directives from above!

Bere Ferrers.

The small village of Bere Ferrers was not always called by this name. It was formerly referred to as Beer Town, and most of the old letters and documents call it such. The first report regarding Beer Town is an unfortunate one, for it relates to the death of the village constable on Christmas Day 1878. The superintendent at the time wrote(7) to the Chief Constable:–

"Sir
I have the honour to report for your information that First Class Constable Number 291 William Gillard, stationed at Beer Town, died on yesterday, the 25th. He had been ill but a short time suffering from inflammation of the lungs. I only received the report of his death this morning as I was leaving Tavistock for Lifton and, fearing I would not return in time to write to you, I telegraphed you. Constable Gillard leaves a widow and four children.
I have the honour to be, Sir
Your obedient servant
William Mitchell
Supt."

Superintendent Mitchell was keen to replace Constable Gillard and arranged for 1st Class Constable 126 John Clarke to remove from Mary Tavy to Beer Town. The justification was that(7) "Constable Clarke is an old constable and not strong, and Beer Town would be a much easier station for him than Mary Tavy". It was, however, a few weeks before Clarke took over, and certain sections of the local community took advantage of the lack of a constable. On the 7th January, a few weeks after Gillard's death, Superintendent Mitchell had ridden out to the area to investigate sheep rustling. He refers to the area as 'Beer Ferris', not too dissimilar to its modern name. He took with him Constables Garland of Morwellham and Whimple from Bere Alston, and they surmised that the thefts had, in fact, been committed by people from Plymouth, who must have sailed up the Tamar to commit the crime.

The Beer Town station was situated in the house known as 'Elmwood', leading down from the top part of the village to the area of the quayside. The last constable being stationed here, when the station closed in 1905, was Constable Walter Blee, by which time the village had

Retired Constable Walter Blee on his daughter's wedding day, 1932.

Mrs G. Lugg

become known by its modern name of Bere Ferrers. It was Constable Blee's daughter who, in 1932, married Constable Frank Burrows, who later became sergeant at Yelverton.

Upon closure, the small beat of Bere Ferrers was transferred to the Bere Alston constable, and it remained so until 1971. Then, when the Bere Alston station also shut its doors, both areas were, and still are, served by officers from Tavistock.

Lamerton.

Lamerton had been remarkably well off in the days of the parish constables. Their vestry records show that several men at one time held the post, but things would change once the unpopular, 'new' police force arrived: Lamerton was provided with just the one full-time constable. The removal of the four or five unpaid officials and replacing them with a solitary officer would have been a change resented by many.

The cottage used as the police house was not actually in the village. Instead, it was situated at Rushford, on the new main road which by-passed the village centre, opposite the Rushford Chapel. Who the first constable at Lamerton was is unclear, but in the September of 1882 Superintendent Mitchell requested(7) the following removals:–

The old Lamerton police house, 1995.

Author's collection

"Sir,
I have the honour to submit the following removals for your consideration
and approval – such removals would be to the benefit of the service.
Second Class Constable Yelland from Princetown to Mary Tavy, First Class
Constable Vanstone from Lamerton to Princetown, Second Class Constable
Chane from Tavistock to Lamerton"

Unfortunately, Chane's posting to Lamerton was short-lived. For, on
the 9th March 1884, Superintendent Mitchell announced his death(7) to
the Chief Constable:-

"Tavistock
March 9th 1884
Sir,
I have the honour to report for your information that No. 190 2nd Class
Constable James Chane died this morning at Lamerton. He took cold on
Thursday last and on Friday he had the Doctor. His poor wife only
forwarded the Doctor's Certificate on yesterday. The widow would be glad
if eight constables could be allowed to act as bearers, and unless I hear
from you to the contrary I will detail eight for the duty.
I have the honour to be, Sir,
Your obedient servant
William Mitchell
Supt."

Constable Callard replaced Chane, and in the December of 1890 he
was the subject of a letter from his superintendent at Tavistock. He was
being summonsed to attend the Tavistock court to answer an offence of
trespass in a field at Sydenham Damerell, the field belonging to a farmer
named Cole from the village. The result was unfortunately never noted
by Superintendent Mitchell. Callard, however, remained in post until the
January of 1893, when he was removed to another station elsewhere in
the Devon Constabulary. Perhaps such a removal away from the West
Devon area had been at his own request. For it was Constable Callard of
Lamerton who had been so involved in the investigations into the Peter
Tavy double murder in the November of 1892 (see chapter 14). This case
brought national publicity and even led to the suicide of one of the
villagers involved in the investigation. The toll that the case had on all
involved was made all the worse when the culprit was hanged. Little
wonder then why Callard left the district, his replacement being
Constable 275 George Lang, who removed from Tavistock. It was then,
with Constable Lang, that the 19th century policing of the village drew to
a close.

Within living memory of the most senior of villagers, names such as
Constable Uglow, Constable Berry and Constable Ash succeeded him
until 1922, when the last constable (named Gill) left. The police house
was then disposed of and the Lamerton beat transferred into the hands
of the Whitchurch constable.

The crossroads at the Blacksmith's Arms was used as the conference
point between the Whitchurch beat and Milton Abbot beat. By the time

that the motor car had arrived into the police service the village of Lamerton was being mainly covered by Tavistock officers. Lamerton's demise as a detached beat station was, perhaps, due to its close proximity to Tavistock. The living memories of the locals will soon fade, however, as time takes its toll. The constables of the village will be but names in a book instead of childhood recollections. Indeed, even the whereabouts of the former police house was very nearly lost.

The occasional pedal cycling officer has sometimes strayed to Lamerton, even as late as the 1980s. Perhaps the village residents might have been convinced that the ghost of Constable Chane had returned to haunt his old beat. The reception, however, that this modern-day cycling constable received soon convinced him that he was a welcome sight.

Mary Tavy.

The Mary Tavy beat, situated on the main Tavistock to Okehampton road on the edge of Dartmoor, is without doubt the best documented beat of West Devon. Particularly useful in tracing the area's social history, as well as incidents on the beat, are the superintendent's correspondence book(7) and the last beat book(13) of the Devon Constabulary, added to which Constable Trigger, who was stationed at Mary Tavy from around the turn of the century until the 1920s, when he retired, kept an occurrence book(8). This book was quite supplementary to any other records necessary.

The first dwellings used as police cottages were 'Rose Cottage', situated near the village school, and, latterly, Oakley Cottage, near the village war memorial (this is on the opposite side of the Bal Lane junction, where the last traditional style Devon police house stands).

One of the first incidents that Superintendent Mitchell was sent to take command of was a report of a man being killed on Blackdown, near Mary Tavy, by a lightning strike. It was in the September of 1878 that he had to ride out from Tavistock to make his enquiries, but it seems that he was sent on a fool's errand. The same superintendent often made visits to the rural areas on the edge of Dartmoor to inspect the mines, which were prolific in the area in the 19th century. On one such visit in the early January of 1880, he reported(7) that he had found "forty-four pounds of blasting powder stored at Wheal Friendship Mine in an unauthorised place". The mine captain was brought to task over the matter, but such incidents were not rare. It was about this time that Constable Kemp was stationed in the village. His name is mentioned in an allegation of bribery when it was suggested that he had been given beer at the Royal Standard public house by a local horse dealer. Upon investigation, it seems that the allegation was malicious, for Kemp was actually buying a pony from the dealer; constables of the day were, it seems, fair game to have complaints made about their sobriety and trustworthiness. Serious crime was a rarity in the day, so when Kelly House at nearby Kelly village was burgled in the November of 1881 all the stops were pulled out – Sergeant Holland of Lifton, along with Constables Cardew of Milton Abbot and Kemp of Mary Tavy, all investigated the case. It transpired, however, that great suspicion rested with the local gardener, and it seems that the matter was resolved without further trouble.

Constable Kemp remained at Mary Tavy until the September of 1882, when he was replaced by 2nd Class Constable Yelland of the Princetown beat. It was Constable Yelland who was the local officer at Mary Tavy at the time of the double murder at Peter Tavy in the November of 1892 (dealt with in chapter 14). What effect this incident had upon him personally is not known but, like many of the other officers locally involved in the investigations, he was moved within two months – to Bere Alston: he was to swap beats with Constable Melhuish, who took over the Mary Tavy station.

Constable Melhuish's replacement was Constable Trigger, who was moved from the Milton Abbot beat, where he had seen out the last years of the 19th century. The exact date is not known, but Constable Trigger was certainly at the Mary Tavy beat by around 1904, as a photograph of him outside of the local village methodist chapel was taken in the period

Wesleyan Chapel, Marytavy

Constable Thomas Trigger of Mary Tavy, c1905.

G. Sargeant

of 1904 to 1907. This, in fact, can be verified from the headgear of the constable for, between these two dates, the relationship between Great Britain and our Germanic cousins was a little strained and the distinctive Prussian pickelhaub helmets worn by the constables of the Devon Constabulary were changed to the unpopular Boer War style bush hats. The Devon Constabulary, incidentally, was one of only three forces in the country to use this type of hat during this period.

Constable Trigger's occurrence book(8) makes particularly interesting reading as a social record of the life of the village between 1911 and 1913. The various incidents dealt with by Constable Trigger in these years leading up to the war give a wonderful impression of rural policing of the day. On 16th April 1911, for example, he caught a Devonport dockyard worker fishing in the River Burn with an ash stick and earth worm, having caught "a fine trout before my very eyes", Trigger reported(8). The man, of course, denied any involvement in the poaching and was subsequently cautioned. As for the "fine trout" (long since dead by then), the good constable ensured that it was "properly treated". What was meant by this can only be surmised at, but surely not too difficult a question to answer in the circumstances! Many of his more mundane incidents involved animals and offences by farmers, work that took him many miles over the moors. On one such occasion he even marched up to the top of Tavy Cleave in order to deal with a pony with a broken leg – something his constabulary successors would only consider, perhaps, with either a Landrover or helicopter!

Trigger duly records his points made with neighbouring constables with copper-plate efficiency. Constable Churchill of the Horrabridge beat made regular points with Trigger at Moorshop Cross, rain or shine. Moorshop Cross is an isolated spot on the edge of the moors and some distance for both men to march. It was, however, a valuable meeting, for their discussions about local criminals travelling their beats was essential to the policing of the area. Fortunately for their modern-day counterpart, the telephone seems to do the job with much greater ease on boot leather. It was, however, not all animals and poaching in the village for Constable Trigger(8). One night he was called to the Royal Standard inn when the landlord alleged that his wife had attempted to cut his throat with a razor. It transpired that the landlord had attempted to do this himself in a bid to take his life. Upon failing to achieve his objective, he blamed his wife! The subsequent enquiries revealed the truth of the matter and no action followed.

Trigger's duties were not always easy, but not too dissimilar to the modern officer of today. For, in the February of 1913, he attended the death of an infant in a cot at Peter Tavy village. His report details his enquiries and the fact that he had to travel at once to Stonehouse in order to report the death to the coroner. Communications in our modern times are taken so much for granted, and a constable of today can only

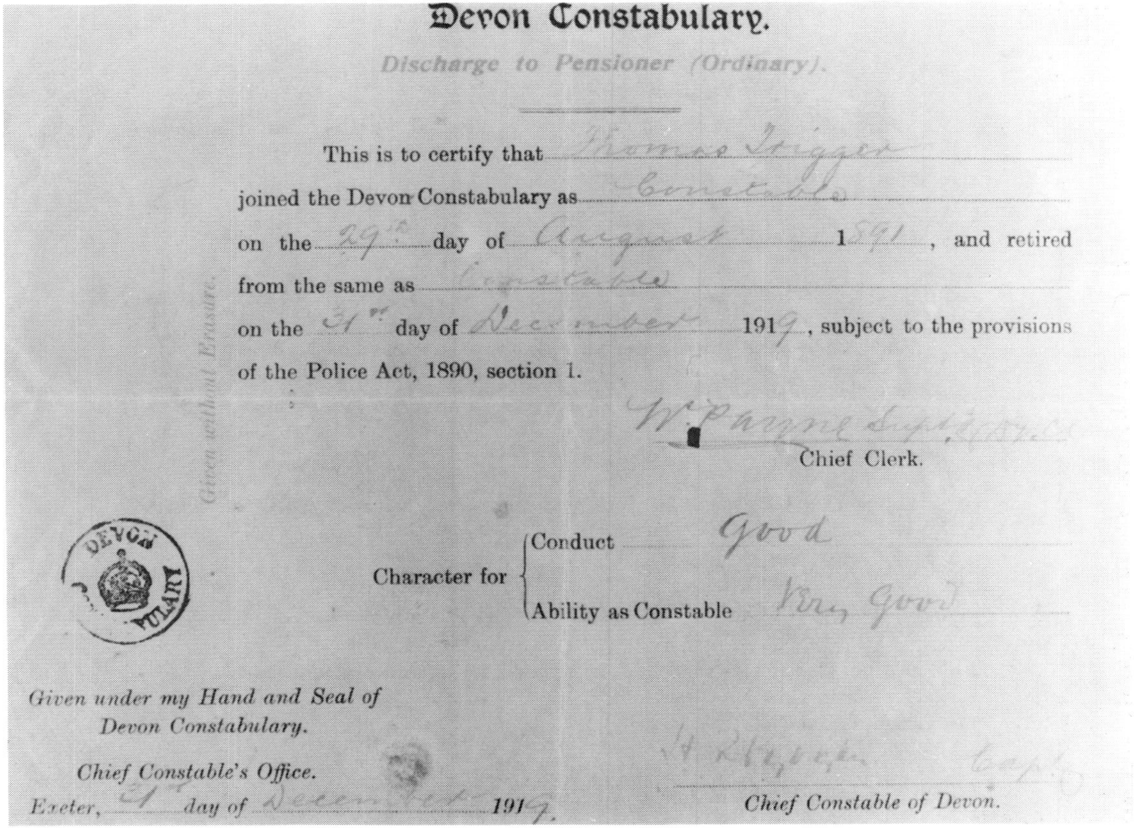

Devon Constabulary.

Discharge to Pensioner (Ordinary).

This is to certify that _Thomas Trigger_ _Constable_

joined the Devon Constabulary as _Constable_

on the _29th_ day of _August_ 18_71_, and retired

from the same as _Constable_

on the _3rd_ day of _November_ 191_9_, subject to the provisions

of the Police Act, 1890, section 1.

W. Pennington

Chief Clerk.

Character for { Conduct _Good_

{ Ability as Constable _Very Good_

Given under my Hand and Seal of
Devon Constabulary.

Chief Constable's Office.

Exeter, _4_ day of _December_ 191_9_.

H. Trigger Capt

Chief Constable of Devon.

Constable Trigger's Discharge Certificate, 1919. *G. Trigger*

85

guess at the efforts that his 'constabulary ancestors' took in undertaking their day to day duties. Other matters, too volumous to mention here, received the attention of Constable Trigger, but on the last day of 1919, after 28 years service, he retired and was issued with his discharge certificate. His pensionable years were then spent at Standard Court, Mary Tavy, not far from the Royal Standard inn, the location of some of his more interesting cases.

Trigger was subsequently replaced by Constable 77 John Body, the first officer to occupy the new police house opened on the 1st October 1930, next to the war memorial. It was Constable Body who enjoyed the luxury of the first telephone in the station when 'Mary Tavy 22' was connected to the house, followed shortly, in 1934, by electric light. Such luxuries made him the envy of his colleagues in those times, and he remained at the village until 1936, when Constable 281 'Paddy' Brettell took over the beat.

Brettell was newly married, his former station being as the single man at Yelverton. He was the son of a tea planter and used to a life a little different than that which might reasonably be expected for a constable of the time. At the Mary Tavy police house he is reported to have had a maid who would answer the door to visitors. One such visitor requested to see the constable, so the maid duly advised the caller that she would "enquire if the master was at home". The caller politely advised the maid that "If her master would be so kind as to come to the door, his Superintendent would like to speak with him!"

Constable Brettell stayed until 1940 and then left the area, only to return in the 1950s as inspector at Tavistock. His replacement was Constable 407 Cyril Anstey, who moved from the Cheriton Fitzpaine station. He remained for the war years at the beat, then Constable 287 Arthur Horwood moved down from Barnstaple to take over the station. His 7-year stay ended in 1952, when Constable 12 Harold Chapman replaced him. He, in turn, only stayed for two years, and Constable 556 Ken Bennett took over until 1959. However, the policeman whom most of the older residents of the village still remember with great affection is John Hurn, Constable 624. Known kindly as 'Long John' because of his great height (he stood well over six feet), John rode a cycle which had to be made especially for him, for he could not ride anything smaller! He arrived at the beat with two years service and was renowned for his immaculate plan drawing, a reputation which lasted well into the 1970s until he retired. It was John Hurn who would attend most of the murders and serious incidents on his cycle in order to to draw plans for the coroner, or court cases, with great accuracy.

His beat book(13) was inherited from his predecessors. It was, however, discontinued in the May of 1965 when, as was the case with all the other country beats, the Chief Constable ordered the end of these invaluable records. Up until then the book had been religiously kept for

Constable John Hurn of Mary Tavy, 1960.

Mrs V. Hurn

34 years by all the constables of Mary Tavy. The crimes recorded therein would not amount to more than thirty in any year but, nevertheless, the constable provided a reassuring figure in the community. The majority of incidents refer to road accidents and animals being knocked down, something which the Dartmoor commoners of today can readily identify with. Retired policemen bemoaned the passing of the beat book as one of the great traditions of the service lost for ever. They have, in a way, been replaced with computer records and criminal intelligence officers. Nevertheless, the day that the beat book was taken away was like a chapter in the tradition of the constabulary banging shut for the stalwarts of the force.

When the Lydford station closed in 1966 it was decided that the Mary Tavy constable would be issued with a motorcycle and cover the two beats. Constable Hurn, though, had other plans. He did not intend to ride a motorcycle for anyone, preferring instead to stay with his bicycle. He was, therefore, faced with a choice: stay and ride a motorcycle or swap with Constable 56 Roger Catterall of Bere Alston, who still covered the Bere peninsular by cycle. Constable Catterall was keen to take over a larger, motorcycle beat, so they eventually exchanged, and Constable Hurn kept his beloved pedal cycle. Constable Catterell, meanwhile, was

Constable Roger Catterall of Mary Tavy, 1965.

Ret'd Sgt R. Catterall

to remain at the Mary Tavy beat until the February of 1971 when it, too, shut its doors. He then removed to South Devon, and the Mary Tavy area was, thereafter, covered by a car from Tavistock station under the new 'panda car' scheme, more popularly known as the 'unit beat policing' system.

One of the last stations to close, Mary Tavy, nevertheless, retained a community constable on a motorcycle until well into the 1980s, in the guise of Constable Tony Bolt, a former Cornwall Constabulary officer. It was the arrival of the new Police and Criminal Evidence Act of 1984 that persuaded him that the day of the police service of his era was drawing to a close. Like the Mary Tavy beat he covered, he, too, became but a memory of yesterday's policing.

Morwellham.

The need for a constable stationed at this busy and thriving port was evident from the start. With public houses in abundance and many miners and dock workers to control, the constable had his work cut out. The earliest recorded name of the local constable is John Halse, who is shown in the 1861 census(3) as occupying number 26 Morwellham. This building is the cottage attached to what is now the shop next to the Ship Inn at the port, and he lived there with his wife and four children. No

The old Morwellham police house, 1994.
Author's collection

doubt his time at Morwellham was made the more memorable because of the events of the 3rd March 1866. It was then that a great uprising occurred at the Devon Great Consuls Mine in the Tamar Valley(14). The miners were supported by reinforcements from their Cornish compatriots until over 2,000 men took part in the disturbances. As a result, constables from all over Devon were drafted in until over 260 officers were at the scene and being supported by 150 soldiers, along with Royal Marines standing by on the Tamar. The troubles eventually died down without loss of life, and peace was restored to this corner of the county.

The 1871 census still shows Halse as the constable, now with an additional two children. Halse, however, was replaced sometime afterwards, and by 1881 Constable John Garland was in the station, along with his family.

Garland seems to have been a most cosmopolitan man for these Victorian times. Although he was a Devon man, having been born in

Highampton, his wife, Annie, was a Scotswoman from Glasgow. He had emigrated to the U.S.A. and both his daughter, Jennie, and his son, Loveday-Scott, were born in Pennsylvania, a great mining area; one can only surmise as to his occupation when in America. Another daughter (also called Annie), on the other hand, was born in Tavistock in 1879, so it seems that the promise of a new life in the States was not to the liking of the Garland family. Whatever, Superintendent Mitchell's records show Garland as still being stationed at Morwellham in the January of 1883, living in the rented cottage next to the Ship Inn. When he left is not known, but he was replaced by Constable Ediford.

By 1888 it was again time for a change. Constable Ediford was removed from Morwellham to Tavistock, and Constable Bright swapped to replace him. A year later, for no recorded reason, Bright was again on the move, this time from Morwellham to Horrabridge station: he changed with Constable Jones. How long Jones stayed is uncertain, but he was succeeded by Constable Crispin, who was to witness the first closure of a police station in West Devon. On 18th November 1891 Superintendent Mitchell wrote(7) thus to the Chief Constable:-

"Sir
I have the honour to suggest the removal of the Morwellham constable to Tavistock for the following reasons. There is very little left of mining at Morwellham and very few miners working there and the constable is very little needed. Secondly another constable is very much needed in Tavistock to do duty in the suburbs of the town and the country beat at night.
I have the honour to be
Sir
Your obedient servant
William Mitchell, Superintendent."

And so, by the end of 1891, this little station had closed and Morwellham came under the responsibility of the Bere Alston constable. It remained so for another 80 years until progress again overtook the area. Constable Crispin was removed to Princetown to replace Constable Cardew, who was retiring. And so ended a chapter in the history of this mining port and that of the Devon Constabulary.

Princetown.

The Princetown beat was the last in the West Devon area to be taken over by Tavistock station, which, perhaps, was an indication of the importance of this outpost. In fact, it was not until 1994 that the front door of the Princetown police house was finally locked and an era in the policing of Dartmoor ended. Up until then there had only ever been two police houses in the village throughout the 140 years of policemen being there, the first being opposite the village school and now called 'The Olde Police Station Cafe', in Tavistock Road. Little do the customers know of the stories that this building could tell whilst they sit enjoying their fish and chips!

From the time when Princetown was built it had been recognised that a police presence would be essential to the well-being of the community. Its policemen, over the decades, have seen a very hard existence in this, the largest single beat in England. The area covered by the solitary constable in the village covered almost 60,000 acres, mostly of remote and inhospitable moorland. The officer of the 19th century on this moorland beat had enough to put up with in the normal course of his duties without the harshness of his senior officers. The very first recorded(7) visit by Superintendent Cornwall in the May of 1875 is a typical example of the austere existence that the constable of the day had:-

"Tavistock, 7th May 1875
Sir
I have the honour to report that upon making my usual visit to the station at Princetown on the 5th April I found the paint on doors etc very dirty, and outside the back door a pool of dirty water covered by slops from the house being thrown there, although the sink is only about four feet from the door. I called the attention of the constable's wife to the dirty state of the walls and paint and also to the pool of dirty water and reminded her that I had found it necessary to speak of the dirty conditions I had found the station in on several occasions; and that I must have the quarters kept in better order. She then became very insolent, told me that I always found fault every time I came and that she kept it cleaner than those who were in it before, and that she could not prevent her children from touching the walls and paint, and a great more which I forget. I told her that she was very insolent and that it is my duty to see that the quarters were properly kept and that I should insist on it being done. Her husband repeatedly told her to go in and be quiet but without avail. Under the circumstances I beg to suggest the desirability of removing this Constable to another station."

Within a short time a replacement constable had arrived, but it seems that the house used as the station was to be a great source of problem and discomfort for every subsequent occupant until the new station was built almost 80 years later. Meanwhile, it was 4 years after, almost to the day, that Cornwall's successor, Superintendent Mitchell, paid a visit to the village station – on horseback. What he found prompted his complaints to the Chief Constable in respect to the cells there: the smell from the sewer in one of the cells was overpowering and damaging the health of the constable and his family.

At around this time Princetown village was an expanding community. The prison provided much source of attention for the constable, but the building of the railway was a greater problem for, whilst it brought a great deal of work into the village, a huge quantity of navvies arrived, along with their inevitable drinking sessions and disorderly behaviour.

Superintendent Mitchell was called up to the village two days after Christmas in 1882, when the navvies committed the most serious of disorders. Urgently writing to the Chief Constable from Princetown, he said(7):-

"There was a disturbance caused by drunken navvies here last evening, when Number 8, First Class Constable James Vanstone was assaulted and injured (the top of his nose was bitten off). One prisoner was locked up, several warders assisted the constable. Constable Vanstone telegraphed to me this morning and I rode away within 10 minutes. On the moor I met the sergeant taking the prisoners in a conveyance to Tavistock, the fog was so thick that I could scarcely see the conveyance. It was raining and the wind was blowing so that when I stopped we could scarcely hear each other's voices. Not long after the sergeant left me he was met by a number of navvies who took the horse by the head, rescued the prisoners, badly assaulted the sergeant and made off across the moors. The sergeant came on to Princetown and had his wounds dressed. I then telegraphed in every direction. One of the men who assisted in the rescue is called "Norrish" a respectable looking navvy and will know the moor as a poacher. He is in dark jacket and cap, with breeches and leggings – no whiskers. The sergeant had taken Constable Simpson from Princetown several miles with him and then had sent him back to do duty at Princetown for the day. As soon as I received Constable Vanstone's telegraph I sent down to Horrabridge for Constable Jones to go to Princetown. I telegraphed to Tavistock for more men and they have arrived (four) at 4.15p.m. The Governor of the Prison would not allow two warders to go with the police to search. The Doctor will not allow the Sergeant to leave until tomorrow. The navvies appeared to have threatened Constable Vanstone and on yesterday several hundred marched about the streets to annoy him but he never sent me word of anything. From what I have been told I fear for the life of Vanstone and I thought it better to ask you for help."

Superintendent Mitchell was required to squash rumours which abounded that he had armed his officers. He was, however, grateful to the Chief Constable for sending down two young constables to be stationed in the village for some time until everything settled. Another constable, stationed at Lifton, was also temporarily removed there to assist, although it was hoped that the railway would be opened in the following summer and that all their troubles would soon be over. The problems following this incident immediately after Christmas 1882, however, were not all as a result of the navvies' behaviour. The Chief Constable refused to pay the "extortionate" doctor's bill for attending Constable Vanstone, and, offered two shillings and sixpence or nothing!

It seems that most of the constables in the Tavistock division were at some stage involved in the incident. Constable Garland of Morwellham pursued several of the escaping navvies across the Tamar to Calstock, and Constable Glanfield of Tavistock travelled a long way into Cornwall in an effort to capture several of Sergeant Richard's assailants. They were all eventually caught and brought to justice but, unfortunately, Sergeant Richards of Tavistock had to be retired from the force as a result of his injuries, and Constable Vanstone was removed out of harm's way from Princetown. Thereafter, the village settled again and life returned to as normal as possible. Superintendent Mitchell, however, continued with his fight for better conditions for the Princetown man. His record book shows that he was a tireless campaigner against the squalid conditions that the village station provided for its constable. Even so, little, it seems, was done to relieve the situation.

The years after the Great War saw the prison used to house prisoners from the political trouble and conflict in Ireland. There was a great deal of worry and it was decided that the constable stationed in the village ought to be supplemented with a second officer. This second constable was to be a single man and he would work a split shift, involving four hours day duty and four hours night duty patrolling the perimeter of the prison walls. A Princetown family called the Worths provided lodgings for him: a name famous on Dartmoor with historians, the Worth family was one of the oldest in the area. The married officer in the house, meanwhile, worked his usual shift.

It was regarded as a privilege for the Princetown man to work a discretionary duty. All his other colleagues, in well-supervised beats, were committed to set hours, but he had a free reign. The married officer acted as the supervisor in a way for the younger single man, who was required to cycle the beat over the moors and to make points. His pedal cycle took him to the Warren House Inn, or to Merrivale, to meet with the Tavistock sergeant – something which would cause gasps from the modern-day Tavistock constable! The village was also regarded as a 'promotion station', with most officers being promoted away from the area. One can only assume that this was a reward for such a harsh posting.

The last of the unmarried officers at the village was Constable Charlie Battershill, who, when World War II broke out, joined up and served with the R.A.F. However, when hostilities ceased, he returned to the police force and was posted back to Princetown, only this time as the married officer and as a replacement for Constable Dave Tancock, who had sadly died at the station following an illness. Incidentally, it was Dave's son, Mike, who was later to be stationed at Yelverton during his time in the division in the late 1950s. Indeed, this situation of sons following in their fathers' footsteps seemed to be quite a trend for the men of the Devon Constabulary and results in the same surnames cropping up time and time again. Charlie Battershill's son, however, never actually became a constable, although he did join the constabulary in later years – in the buildings department. Meanwhile, it was Charlie who was the first constable to wear the new open-necked tunic of the police whilst he was at the village station – the most significant change in uniform since 1856, when the police service in Devon was formed. It was also Charlie who campaigned for a new police house in the village for many years until, finally, in 1953, and after living in the old building for so long, his dream came true. Even then, the actual construction of the new police house – to the typical pattern of the modern police house in the Devon Constabulary – had not been completed without its problems as it had proved necessary to sink the foundations to a depth of 8 feet in order to find solid footing, due to the nature of the ground upon which it was built. Moreover, the unexpectedly high building costs resulted in the proposal to build a second property on the site in Tavistock Road – for the district nurse – having to be 'put on hold'.

Many officers followed Constable Battershill, and Princetown policing moved into a new era. Constable Colin Evans arrived in the mid-1960s, but he did not stay long, either at Princetown or in the rank, for he retired as Assistant Chief Constable of South Wales. Perhaps his time at this lonely Devon outpost bode well for him.

Constable Derek Roper with the actor James Ellis (Inspector Bert Lynch from 'Z Cars'), 1966.

Ret'd Supt D. Roper

Constable Derek Roper arrived after Evans in 1966. He came from a long line of Devon Constabulary officers as illustrated by the fact that in 1950 three brothers and a sister from this family had held the ranks of superintendent, inspector, sergeant, and constable, whilst the inspector's son was a cadet in the force. It was also one of the Roper family who had been involved in the trials of the 1932 mutineers at Princetown, and even to this day a member of the family is still serving in the Devon & Cornwall Constabulary.

In the five years that Derek Roper was at Princetown he saw many significant changes, the greatest of these being the introduction of a beat vehicle. Until then, the officer at the station had been paid an allowance for using his own car. The first vehicle used at Princetown was a mini-moke. Able to cover the beat on and off the moors, it was a useful resource and one that the innovative Constable Roper used to great effect. On one occasion, following a search, he located a suicidal man on the moors, who had taken a cocktail of pills. Realising that he needed to find some quick way of making him ill, Constable Roper then tried pouring the contents of the mini-moke's windscreen-washer bottle down the throat of the unsuspecting man hell-bent on doing away with himself! It had the desired effect, for the man survived both the pills and the contents of the bottle – the day had been saved.

One of the greatest break-outs in the history of the prison took place whilst Constable Roper was at the station. This involved Frank Mitchell (the 'Mad Axeman'), who was assisted in his bid for freedom by some of his associates in London. In fact, it was Constable Roper's wife who recalls taking the message from the prison to announce the escape, which also serves to illustrate that the constable's wife of the 1960s played as important a role in the police service as her predecessor of the 19th century.

Constable Roper was subsequently promoted away from Princetown and replaced by an officer removed up from Tavistock. That officer was Constable Steer-Kemp, and he arrived in 1971. He then became as much a familiar figure in his Landrover as his predecessor until he, too, was promoted away and replaced by Constable Privett. Later, in the early 1980s, Constable Chris Hucker took over, his wife coming from a local family at Buckland. Friendly accommodation was always provided for the night at this remote station to a 'snowed-in' constable on a trip from Tavistock, as several officers would recall, but it was the snow that was to provide the greatest consternation to the Hucker family. With drifts blocking the roads to the village, and the constable's wife in labour, the prison hospital prepared itself for the first baby to be born within its walls. The snows abated, however, and young Miss Hucker avoided the indignity of having 'Dartmoor Prison' recorded as being her place of birth on her certificate!

Constable Simon Raeburn took over the beat in 1984 and, along with his variety of livestock, remained there some years. It had always been somewhat of a tradition for the village officer to have a sheep or two, or the odd pony, in the garden. It was accepted as part of the role of the beat officer. His duties on the moors took him into contact with many incidents involving animals on the moors, and it was inevitable that he would become a smallholder in his off duty-hours.

The last officer was Constable Dave Folland. Also keen on livestock, he remained in the house until the closure of the beat station in 1994. The house was then sold, and Constable Folland went to Plymouth city to work. So the last of the country stations in West Devon shut its door

Constable Simon Raeburn of Princetown, 1985.

The Police Review/S. Raeburn

on almost one and a half centuries of continual policing. The presence of a policeman in the village still remains with an officer from Tavistock specifically allocated the moorland beat to patrol by Landrover. What the officers of this remote and harsh little village in the middle of the moors had to contend with we can only guess, but one thing is for sure – living in such a close community in such isolated conditions meant that few other constables lived and breathed their work every day as much as those at Princetown did.

Whitchurch.

To a tourist passing on his way through West Devon, Whitchurch might well be mistaken as being one and the same town as Tavistock. Anyone from Whitchurch will tell you differently. It is within living memory that Tavistock and Whitchurch village were separate communities with fields and farmland between them. Modern-day housing has filled that gap, but its identity, fortunately, remains.

When it came to the policing of Whitchurch, it certainly did have its own identity as the old village stocks, now preserved in the churchyard,

Whitchurch parish stocks, 1995.

stand witness. In fact, the village also had its own police house and constable, although it was not until after Superintendent Mitchell had arrived on the scene that Whitchurch could boast its own station. He clearly felt that the area was sufficiently busy to warrant a permanent police presence in the village, and it is evident that the constable, coming under the sergeant at Tavistock, had an important role there. Interestingly enough, the house was not actually owned by the police authority. Instead, it was rented from the Highman family of Whitchurch and is the cottage now known as number 182 Whitchurch Road.

Superintendent Nicholls followed the example of his predecessor and never left Whitchurch without a constable for very long. In the September of 1892 he wrote(7) to the Chief Constable one of his usual letters suggesting removals:–

"Tavistock
September 1892
'Suggested removals'
Sir,
I have the honour to suggest for your consideration the following removal, which I consider would be for the benefit of the service by Constable Andrews from Bridestowe to Tavistock with Constable Holwill from Tavistock to Bridestowe. Also Constable Hilman from Whitchurch to Chillaton with Constable Cox from Chillaton to Tavistock and a recruit sent from Headquarters to Whitchurch.
I have the honour to be, Sir
Your obedient Servant
R. Nicholls
Supt."

97

The last officer to live in the rented house was a Constable Nankivell, in the years between the two wars. With the increased development of the area, new estates were being built in the land between village and town, and when houses at Crelake Park were constructed by the local authority, it was decided to rent one of them for the Whitchurch constable. As a result, the old cottage went back into the hands of the Highman family and, on 12th October 1926, Constable 361 Ernest Bedford was removed from Bideford to take over the Whitchurch beat in the new police house, situated at the corner of Whitchurch Road and Crelake Park. Although only a stone's throw away from Tavistock police station, this constable was still responsible for the Whitchurch beat and no doubt, at times of trouble, he would be the first to be called upon by his inspector at Tavistock.

At this point it should be mentioned that the beat of the Whitchurch constable from the early 1920s also included the village of Lamerton, following the closure of the police house there in 1922. Consequently, his duties were even more onerous than those of his predecessors, particularly as regards having to make points. One such point was on the edge of his beat at the Dartmoor Inn (Merrivale), which involved a stiff walk across the moors in a police helmet and cape that would often be no match against the weather on Dartmoor. Imagine, then, his feelings when, having arrived there and waited the statutory 15 minutes, his sergeant failed – as would sometimes be the case – to turn up! This, however, had to be accepted as just being part of the job for if a constable failed to make his point he risked serious disciplinary action from his sergeant, who had the list of points that a constable was due to make on a particular day.

It also befell the Whitchurch constable to make the Warren Cross point when a convict had escaped from Dartmoor Prison. Often this would mean staying out all night, and highlights, yet again, the harshness of the duties of the early constable. Another long trek, meanwhile, was to The Blacksmith's Arms at Lamerton, on the other side of his beat, where he would make a conference point with the Milton Abbot constable. What involvement the nearby local licensee had in this conference point is kept a closely guarded secret!

In 1933 the Whitchurch beat was taken over by Constable 174 Fred Connett, who arrived in the September of that year to replace Constable Bedford, who, in turn, was posted to Tavistock. Like many of his colleagues, Fred had joined the Devon Constabulary in the years prior to the Great War of 1914 and had subsequently 'joined up' to do his duty. Police constables were allowed to join the services on the basis that their peace-time posts would be held for them should they return from the war – unfortunately many never came home again. Fred actually joined the police battery at Bristol with his great friend Constable Bertie Waterson, and they went off to France together to serve with the men of

The men of the Devon Constabulary, 1914. Included in the photograph is Constable Fred Connett (back row – thrid from left)

D. Connett

99

the Devon Constabulary in the Heavy Regiment Royal Garrison Artillery. Whilst there, Fred suffered greatly from the trials of the trenches and was later returned to England with bronchitis. But then, after recovering, he served at Ypres, where he was awarded with the Distinguished Conduct Medal.

Constable Connett's arrival at the Whitchurch beat was actually some 2 years before the nation was celebrating the silver jubilee of the reign of King George V. It was amidst these celebrations that a march took place and several functions occurred in Tavistock town, during which he was photographed marching down Plymouth Road to the Meadows with his inspector, Mr Barnicoat, and Sergeant Gale from Tavistock. His two Tavistock colleagues also accompanied him, and they were to be present

The Tavistock force out on parade in 1935, with Inspector Barnicoat accompanied by Sergeant Gale and Constables Connett, Pollard and Marshall.

D. Connett

at the opening of the new bridge spanning the canal and an archway on the river walk beside the Tavy.

Constable Connett remained at Whitchurch until retiring in 1938. His retirement was not to last long, however: the Second World War brought about many retired men returning for active duty in the constabulary as first reserve officers, and he was to carry on in uniform way past the retiring age for a constable. In the meantime, his replacement at Whitchurch was Constable 152 Arthur Walters. Arthur's son Dennis, in true Devon Constabulary tradition, also became a constable and served, amongst other places, at the Bridestowe beat in the 1950s. Arthur, on the other hand, had been posted from the Crabtree beat, now long since demolished under the development of the Marsh Mills area between Plymouth and Plympton.

The surviving beat book of the Whitchurch station is a fine specimen of copper-plate accuracy and meticulous recording of daily noteworthy events in the area. Included in its pages is reference to a busy period for the constable with respect to road accidents arising from the increased use of motor cars. It also reminds us, amongst other things, that Gulworthy Cross was within the beat, a location that must have taken some time to reach by cycle for the poor Whitchurch policeman.

The last officer to be stationed at the Whitchurch beat was Constable John Cuttle. It was then officially closed and amalgamated with the Tavistock town section as there seemed little use in having a dedicated constable for an area that had, effectively, been swallowed up by the sprawling town of Tavistock. The police house, though, was not dispensed with until the late 1950s, being used latterly to house subsequent Tavistock officers, so it was not until then that the story of the Whitchurch beat finally came to an end.

✳ ✳ ✳ ✳ ✳

Chapter 9

THE LIFTON SECTION

Lifton Station.

The old Lifton station was situated in what is now the Courthouse Bar of the Arundell Arms Hotel, on the main road through the village. The quarter sessions court stood between the houses of the constable and the sergeant, and the enquiry office was positioned in what would have been the sergeant's front room. The sergeant of police at Lifton had a

Lifton police station and court, 1949.
Author's collection

rather raw deal from the start, however. It was in the March of 1888 that Superintendent Mitchell pleaded with the Chief Constable:—(7) "Lifton Station requires immediate repairs in many places. The kitchen range is worn out and the sergeant has to send his dinner to the bakehouse to be cooked". Again, the following February, in 1889, he states that(7) "The chimneys at Lifton station are in a dangerous condition and likely to fall". Such was the condition of the place that Constable Perkins could not light a fire to warm his family in winter. It was, perhaps, a blessing that he was posted to Bratton Clovelly the following year and replaced by Constable Melhuish. The sergeant did not stay long, either, perhaps because of the condition of the house, for in the May of 1891 a suggested replacement was being proposed for him: Superintendent Mitchell was recommending promotion for 1st Class Constable 91 Cardew from Princetown to sergeant at Lifton. Cardew was well thought of, he had 26 years service and was a good scholar. He was, however, much wiser than the superintendent had bargained for. Upon hearing of the possible move to Lifton, albeit with promotion, he promptly retired!

Sergeant Vanstone was next to take over the station. A subsequent sergeant was Edward Ball, Sergeant No. 227. He was posted to Lifton in 1903 and remained there until he retired in the October of 1920 with 34 years service. During the ensuing years, the establishment at the village was increased to a sergeant with two constables, Archie Fry being one such constable, who stayed for some years at the beat as senior constable. He was assisted by a single man, who resided in lodgings in the village.

By 1940 the sergeant at Lifton was Sergeant 88 Jim Perryman. Like many of his colleagues he had come from a policing family; his father had served in the Devon Constabulary, and, in turn, his sons both

Constable Edward Ball, 1888.
Mrs T. Grunnell, Launceston, Tasmania

103

became constables, making the family contribution to the force a total of over 100 years. Previously, Sergeant Perryman had served through the whole of the Great War from the age of fifteen, fighting at the Somme and Ypres, where he had been awarded the Distinguished Conduct Medal. Whilst at Lifton he was responsible for 'keeping an eye' on Haile Selassie, the Emperor of Ethiopia, who stayed at the Arundell Arms for some time during his exile.

The war years provided a degree of excitement at the beat for in 1941 incendiary bombs were dropped around the village in an attempt to destroy fields of crops before the harvest. Constable Ron Honeywill was stationed with Sergeant Perryman at the time, and received a report of an unexploded bomb in one such field some miles away. He cycled off and returned to his sergeant some hours later with it in his raincoat pocket! He then continued to his house at the station and placed it on the kitchen table prior to the army bomb squad declaring it to be highly dangerous and dealing appropriately with it. Constable Honeywill later joined up into the special investigation branch of the army for war service, along with the ill-fated Constable Bob Southcott, whose widow took over the Roborough police house when he was killed in Germany.

Lifton station also saw the capture of one of the few escaped German prisoners of war in the area. Sergeant Perryman and War Reserve Constable Maurice Gloyne found the escapee hiding in the gardens of the Arundell Arms Hotel. This was following a series of burglaries all the way from the prison camp at South Brent, from where he had made good his escape, to the final break-in at Sydenham House, not far from Lifton village.

Sergeant Perryman stayed at Lifton until 1953, when he was replaced, subsequently, by Sergeant Len Cloade. It was Sergeant Cloade who saw the last of the old station in the December of 1961 – 12 months after the old magistrates court had held its last hearing under the jurisdiction of Doctor Mary Sutherland, JP. The building, by this time, was in a dreadful state, and a new station was built a few hundred yards down the main road towards Okehampton. The new, small station, with three houses, must have seemed a modern luxury in comparison! It was opened, with much ceremony, by the chairman of the police committee in the presence of the Assistant Chief Constable. The beat officers and special constables were also brought in for the opening, and a proud Sergeant Coade took command of his new station.

The last officer in charge at Lifton was Sergeant Pat Clifford. His position was moved into Tavistock in the late 1960s and the station became a sixteen hour, three man beat. The area was covered by one of the new style cars, and the officers worked a shift of 9am to 5pm, and 5pm to 1am. Constables Mike Nelson, Fred Axworthy and John Daniels were but three such officers. Another, Constable Colin Evans (formerly of the Princetown beat), eventually transferred to the South Wales police and retired as Assistant Chief Constable some years later.

Opening day at Lifton station, 1961 — Sergeant Len Cloade and Assistant Chief Constable Bill Harvey are in the centre of the picture. *J. Spry*

DIVISION OF LIFTON

PARISHES IN THE DIVISION.

BRADSTONE
BRATTON CLOVELLY
BRIDESTOWE
BROADWOODWIDGER
CORYTON

DUNTERTON
GERMANSWEEK
KELLY
LEWTRENCHARD
LIFTON

MARYSTOWE
NORTH PETHERWIN
ST. GILES-IN-THE-HEATH
STOWFORD
THRUSHELTON

VIRGINSTOW
WERRINGTON

JUSTICES ACTING FOR THE DIVISION.

NATHANIEL HEARD, Esq
†*COLIN SPENCER JAMES, Esq
*HERBERT SAMSON BALL, Esq

[*MRS GLADYS LEONORA BRIMACOMBE
JOHN EDMUND G. E. DAWE, Esq.
FRANCIS STANBURY, Esq.

THE CHAIRMAN of the BROAD-
WOODWIDGER RURAL DISTRICT
COUNCIL (A. S. GUBBIN, Esq.)

*JUVENILE COURT PANEL.

†PROBATION CASE COMMITTEE.

SUPPLEMENTAL LIST:—MAJOR C. H. H. CALMADY-HAMLYN.

The following DAYS are appointed for holding **PETTY SESSIONS**
for the year 1954.

SPECIAL SESSIONS BEING PARTICULARISED WHEN ALSO HOLDEN.

PLACE OF MEETING :

PETTY SESSIONAL COURT HOUSE, THE POLICE STATION, LIFTON.

The Business of the Meeting will commence at 10-30 o'clock a.m. precisely.

DAYS APPOINTED.			BUSINESS TO BE DONE.
JANUARY	7th :	THURSDAY	Special Sessions for transfer of Licences ; Appointment of Annual Licensing Meeting; and for General Business. Quarterly Meeting of Probation Case Committee and Juvenile Court Panel.
FEBRUARY	4th :	THURSDAY	Annual Licensing Meeting; and Petty Sessions for General Business.
MARCH	4th :	THURSDAY	Adjourned Licensing Meeting ; and for General Business.
APRIL	1st :	THURSDAY	Petty Sessions for General Business. Quarterly Meeting of Probation Case Committee and Juvenile Court Panel.
MAY	6th :	THURSDAY	Special Sessions for Transfer of Licences ; and for General Business.
JUNE	3rd :	THURSDAY	Petty Sessions for General Business; and for appointment of Probation Case Committee.
JULY	1st :	THURSDAY	Special Sessions for Transfer of Licences ; and for General Business. Quarterly Meeting of Probation Case Committee and Juvenile Court Panel.
AUGUST	5th :	THURSDAY	Petty Sessions for General Business.
SEPTEMBER	2nd :	THURSDAY	Special Sessions for Transfer of Licences; and for General Business.
OCTOBER	7th :	THURSDAY	Petty Sessions for General Business and Quarterly Meeting of Probation Case Committee and Juvenile Court Panel. Election of Chairman and Deputy Chairman for 1955. Appointment of Divisional Licensing Committee for 1955. Appointment of members of the Magistrates' Courts Committee, County Probation Committee and Confirming and Compensation Committee for 1955.
NOVEMBER	4th :	THURSDAY	Special Sessions for Transfer of Licences; and for General Business.
DECEMBER	2nd :	THURSDAY	Petty Sessions for General Business.

Special Sessions for proceedings taken under the Children and Young Persons' Acts 1933 and 1938, will be held on the first Monday in each month, at 10-30 a.m., or by special arrangement.

Petty Sessions under the Provisions of the Magistrates' Courts Act 1952 have been fixed for each of the above-mentioned days and for every other day during the year at 10-30 o'clock a.m.

General Quarter Sessions of the Peace for Devon will be holden at Exeter on Wednesday, 6th January ; Wednesday, 7th April; Wednesday, 7th July ; and Tuesday, 5th October, 1954, at 10-30 a.m.

GEO. G. WILSON,

CLERK TO THE JUSTICES.

Dated 5th November, 1953.

Phone 348.

16, Westgate Street, Launceston.

LAUNCESTON PRINTING COMPANY, LIMITED, 4 RACE HILL,

Gradually, the establishment of three constables reduced until, by the 1990s, only one constable remained. Constable Terry Guest, a former fireman on the local railway, was stationed at Lifton in 1967, and retired as its last constable in 1995, having seen many changes in those decades. 1996 then saw the sale of the station and the beat transferred back into the Tavistock section area from Okehampton. This, in turn, led to Constable Dave Barker taking over as the new community constable, covering the beat by car, and to Lifton station becoming the last detached beat in West Devon to close.

As a postcript it is worth mentioning that because of its locality in West Devon, and having been on the main A30 road, Lifton station had often transferred from one section area into another. In fact, in its time it had been in five different divisions – Plympton, Okehampton, Launceston, Barnstaple and Totnes.

Bratton Clovelly.

The Bratton Clovelly station was about the furthest for the superintendent from Tavistock to ride when checking on his constables. The old station was in amongst the terrace of cottages leading to the public house in the village and was known until recently as 'Inglenook'.

The old Bratton Clovelly police cottage, 1994.
Author's collection

Perhaps because of the distance from Tavistock station and from the sergeant at Lifton, the constable posted to the village had to be a senior and competent man. On the 11th November 1885, the superintendent rode to the village to pay a call on Constable Ediford. Upon arriving at

107

the cottage, to his horror, he found a 'political' poster in the window – a heinous crime for the day. He immediately wrote(7) to the Chief Constable:-

"Sir,
When I was at Bratton Clovelly on Thursday last I found that the Constable had a large printed bill in his window, in the room which I have seen him in at dinner time. The bill said "Liberal Committee Room". I ordered the removal of the bill at once. I found it had been placed there the evening before by the man who rents the room now as an office."

Constable Ediford was, for some reason, soon removed from the village! However, he was not replaced for some time, because in the February of 1888 a man by the name of 'Tickle' made false complaints to the police about having poultry stolen from his yard. The superintendent then ordered Sergeant Stapleton and Constable Guscott of Lifton to make enquiries. They found that the man had made the complaint in order to prove that the village was a crime-ridden and unruly place, and needed a policeman. The superintendent concluded his report(7) thus: "I am of the opinion that Tickle has given all this trouble for the purpose of getting a constable sent to the village. All Tickle's neighbours say the man is a nuisance to the parish." It was true that the residents wanted a constable back, but the superintendent reported that "The district is very quiet and there is no crime". Tickle was, however, successful in getting a replacement, and the villagers were again content – but that contentment became short-lived. Unfortunately, with the railway navvies causing problems at Bere Alston, Constable Avent (the new Bratton Clovelly officer) was removed to offer support to his Bere Alston colleague. The ensuing complaints from the villagers, however, were listened to and Constable Simpson of Chillaton was removed to Bratton Clovelly in order to cover Avent's absence. What Chillaton parish made of this is not known, but Simpson remained at Bratton Clovelly until he retired in 1890.

He was replaced by Constable Perkins, who had been at Lifton. Perkins remained until 1894, when the new superintendent, Nicholls, pleaded for a replacement. He was asked to justify the urgency and stated that "The station is situated eight miles from the sergeant and fourteen from the Superintendent. As such is only suitable for a constable who can be relied upon". No doubt a replacement was found, but little is recorded in documents. Senior residents of the village, however, recall that Constable Lawrence Middlewick, followed by Constable Joe Gater, were the last to be stationed at the old cottage before the new house was built just prior to the start of World War II.

Several constables of the Devon force occupied the new house in subsequent years, and all of them were entrusted to ensure that the relationship between the local Mrs Blagdon and the police was well kept. It was she who owned several tracking bloodhound dogs, which

One of Mrs Blagdon's bloodhounds searching for an escapee, c1955.

Robert Sanderson/Westway Publications

played a major part in the prison escape scheme for Dartmoor prison. It was also her dogs which caught several escapees in the area, so it is true to say that an essential part of the Devon Constabulary's operations actually lived within the beat. As for the officers around this time, Brian Hakeman is mentioned as is Constable Bright, who was subsequently posted to Lydford and replaced by Constable 279 Arthur Seldon. However, Constable Seldon only stayed at Bratton Clovelly for 18 months, before he was also moved to Lydford, to again follow in Constable Bright's footsteps.

After Constable Seldon's departure the beat continued to be manned, in turn, by other constables, one of the last being Constable 288 Dennis Levett, who came from Honiton in the January of 1958. It was his immediate successor, though, who was to be the last beat officer at Bratton Clovelly. This was Constable Keith James, who left in the mid-1960s and later became the North Devon coroner's officer. The Bratton

Clovelly beat was then taken over by the Lewdown constable, while the police house was taken over for the patrol motorcyclist from the Okehampton traffic department, Motor Patrol Constable Mike Conelly. He, in turn, was followed by the last policeman to live there – Motor Patrol Constable Brian Bass.

By the 1970s the police house had been sold and Bratton Clovelly joined many other villages throughout the county to lose their resident policeman.

Bridestowe.

The village station at Bridestowe, situated on the main road running down through the heart of the westcountry, was some way to the north of Tavistock. It was, however, originally within the Tavistock division in the time of Superintendent Mitchell, and it was not until the start of the 20th century that the station transferred into the control of the sergeant at Hatherleigh, within the Okehampton division. The early records of the

Bridestowe police house, c1930.
Mrs I. Pearn

station show 2nd Class Constable 327 John Howard as being the officer stationed at this beat. He died 'in post' on 14th March 1879 from bronchitis, and was sorely missed due to the trouble which was being

Constable Arthur Walters with some of the village children, c1958.

Mrs I. Pearn

experienced with the navvies building the peat railway onto the moors from the village. A replacement was soon found, however.

It was Bridestowe School which featured in a letter(7) from Superintendent Mitchell in the August of 1885, when a pupil suffered from an 'over-zealous' caning by the schoolmaster. Young John Heathman of the village succumbed to his injuries, yet there seemed to be insufficient evidence to draw a warrant for the arrest of the schoolmaster involved, and no further action was taken. Perhaps those of this century who talk of the Victorian 'good old days' might like to reflect on their perception of how it might actually have been.

Little else of note is recorded at the station for several years, other than a theft of a bale of wool investigated by Sergeant Vanstone of Lifton in 1892, and a change of station in the September of that year, when Constable Andrews was removed from Bridestowe and swapped with Constable Holwill of Tavistock. Thereafter, the village soon went into the Okehampton area, and to include much more of the events of the village would poach too far into the story of another division. Suffice to say, the village boasted several police houses over the years, the last being vacated in the late 1960s. Also, during the war years, the constable for the village was Jimmy Green, who had been removed from Yelverton. A single man, he had lived in lodgings, whilst his house was occupied by another officer not connected with the village beat.

In the true spirit of the 'family' of the Devon Constabulary, one constable at the village, Constable 196 Dennis Walters, was the son of Constable Arthur Walters of Whitchurch. As already mentioned, surnames often repeated themselves through generations of proud Devon officers from 'police families'.

Broadwoodwidger.

The station cottage at Broadwoodwidger is first mentioned in a letter from Superintendent Mitchell on the 2nd of February, 1881. He tells the Chief Constable that "Consequent upon your orders for Constable Martin's removal", he had sent to the owner of the cottage in which Constable Martin lived at Broadwoodwidger, to ask if the cottage could be kept, and not rented out, in order that Constable Martin's replacement might reside there. It was suggested that Constable Parr of Tavistock should be removed to the Broadwood beat because he was a native of Tavistock, and, it was "not at all healthy" for a local man to police the area due to familiarity with the public. The cottage used for many years at the village is situated at the rear gate of the churchyard, no longer remembered in the memories of the residents, but passed down from a former generation to children who are now themselves senior citizens.

It was four years later that the superintendent rode out to Broadwood

The old Broadwoodwidger police cottage, 1995.

Author's collection

following allegations and complaints made against the local officer, Constable Gorman. Upon his arrival, the complaints were withdrawn and no further action was taken. It is not known what the nature of the complaints were, nor how or why they were withdrawn. Perhaps it is best not to enquire too deeply!

The Broadwood beat was regarded as a busier one than the neighbouring Bratton Clovelly village. In the October of 1888 the Bratton Clovelly beat was vacant and the Chief Constable was duly told(7) "The Bratton Clovelly beat is covered by the Broadwoodwidger and Lewdown constables. One has five night shifts a month and the other six in the beat. Both visit the parish occasionally by day, the Lewdown constable three or four times a week sometimes." The distances marched by these Victorian constables would put their modern-day counterparts to shame!

The last of these Victorian constables was Constable Bibbings. It was he who, in 1890, had been removed from Lydford to the Broadwood beat. His successor in the early part of this century was the last local officer, and by the Great War the beat had been closed. The constable was subsequently removed to Lifton, whose officers covered Broadwoodwidger from then on. The rented cottage was thus returned to its owner, and its location became but a memory told by a father to a young son who, in turn, fortunately passed it on in his 90th year to an enquiring policeman writing a book.

Chillaton.

The old Chillaton police cottage, 1994.
Author's collection

Chillaton station was within the Lifton sergeant's section. A small cottage was rented for the constable in the village and is now, after much alteration, the first single storey cottage on the left when entering the village from the Tavistock direction. Constable Labdon was stationed there in 1879. It was he who had to travel by train, into Tavistock, in order to present his sickness certificate to his superintendent, barely able to walk through an injury to his leg; he was obliged to use a walking stick. It was, however, felt that if he was fit enough to present himself to the superintendent, he was well enough for duty!

It was not until the February of 1881 that Constable Labdon left the Chillaton beat to move to Lifton. He was then replaced by Constable Simpson, who stayed until the October of 1889, when Superintendent Mitchell was faced with problems from the railway construction navvies. Because of the railway line being built at Bere Alston, the village there became very rowdy and several constables were swapped around to provide reinforcements for the solitary Bere Alston officer. The Bratton Clovelly man, Constable Avent, was a "good strong individual" and "would well suit the Bere Alston navvies", the superintendent told the Chief Constable(7). His station, though, could not be left unguarded, so the more gentle Constable Simpson was removed from Chillaton to the Bratton Clovelly beat to look after the village in Avent's absence. The Chillaton station was, therefore, 'suppressed' for four months: it seems that it was not regarded as a busy station and, so, could manage without a constable for a short time.

As promised, the Chillaton station was again back in business in the February of 1890, but with Constable Avent now housed there in place of Constable Simpson. It is not known what Constable Simpson made of this, but it is understood that Constable Avent was "somewhat weary" after his four months with the Bere Alston navvies, so could do with a quieter station for a few months. What induced this fatigue is not known!

Constable Avent remained for just a few months because, on August 13th 1890, Superintendent Mitchell wrote to the Chief Constable requesting a replacement for the village. If that officer was a single man, the Chief Constable was informed, then suitable lodgings could be provided at ex-Constable Westacott's cottage. (It appears that it was a common practice to lodge single officers with retired policemen at country beats; after all, the police owned few cottages and generally rented accommodation for country stations). A single man arriving in the village, however, brought added responsibility to his landlord, whose house was converted into the village station. As a result, Constable Cox, a married man, was soon stationed at the village (perhaps to the relief of ex-Constable Westacott) and remained until the September of 1892, when he was removed to Tavistock. His replacement was Constable Hilman, who was removed from the Whitchurch beat to the village.

How much longer the station remained open is a little uncertain, but by the mid-1920s, Chillaton had seen the last of its resident constables: the officer was removed into Lifton and from then on the village was covered by the Lewdown beat and, later, the Lifton station.

Ladycross.

The Ladycross beat was a reasonable newcomer to the Devon County Constabulary, the station not being opened until the mid-1930s. Prior to this, the locality had been covered by the North Petherwin beat, under the supervision of the sergeant at Lifton, and one of the first incidents reported in the area(7), of note, had been the accidental death of a quarry worker, James Northey, of Bridgetown at Werrington. He had been tamping gunpowder into a hole at Yeolmbridge quarry on 10th April 1879 when he unfortunately struck the copper tamping rod too firmly, causing an explosion. Superintendent Mitchell of Tavistock had been obliged to ride by horse to the area to investigate the death.

Once the Ladycross house (situated at the top of the hill next to Yeolmbridge Chapel and opposite Werrington School) had been opened, reasonable records were kept and its history is well documented. A number of Devon constables occupied the station in its time, including Coombes, Godfery, Corbett, Fayter and Southcott. Constable 74 Eric

Constable Eric Copin at a village fete, 1950.

E. Copin

Copin was another. He was stationed there in 1948 and remained in post for two years until being removed to the Cornwood beat, near Ivybridge. Eric's father, incidentally, had been a constable at Lewdown during the early part of the century and had retired as superintendent.

Constable Copin had replaced Constable Tapley at the beat, which consisted of 13,500 acres with no public houses to supervise – a real blessing for a policeman! This bonus was soon found to be balanced with other misfortunes: one, for instance, was that the Ladycross constable at the time was the officer chosen to man the distant Warren Cross point, near Tavistock, whenever a prisoner had made a bid for freedom from Dartmoor Prison. Constable Copin also had a number of registered aliens living in the area, namely some German ex-prisoners of war. One such man worked on the large, Werrington estate nearby.

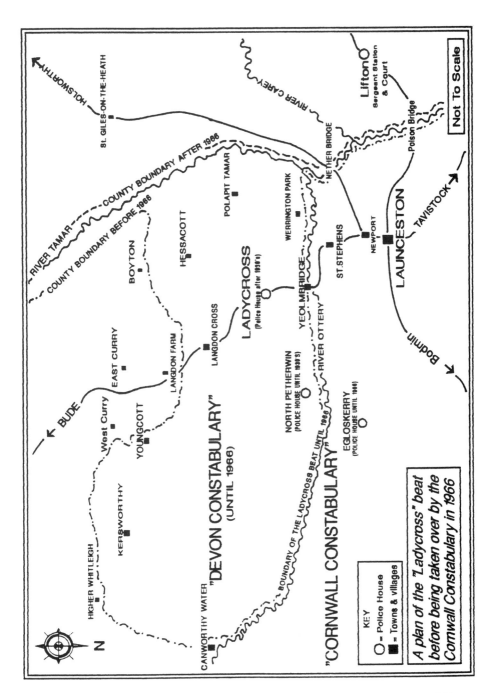

A plan of the "Ladycross" beat before being taken over by the Cornwall Constabulary in 1966

Not To Scale

KEY
○ = Police House
■ = Towns & villages

117

Constable Copin was followed at Ladycross by Bill Maze – and by Mike Brinley, the last Devon constable to be stationed at the house when Cornwall claimed the parishes of North Petherwin and Werrington following the change of county boundaries. It was at midnight on 31st March 1966 that Cornwall took over this odd little lump of Devon. The old police house in the Cornwall station at nearby Egloskerry village had been due for replacement for some years, so it seemed reasonable to amalgamate the two beats and to move the Cornwall officer into the Ladycross house so as to cover both areas from that date. The officer chosen was actually Constable Charles Voakes, and he had obtained

Constable Charles Voakes, 1966.

C. Voakes

special permission to move a day early. Thus his first day's duty as a Cornwall Constabulary officer was to police the Devon parishes of North Petherwin and Werrington, and to supervise the Devon special constabulary sergeant manning the polling station at the local school. A motorcycle was issued to the enlarged beat – the old BSA from the Egloskerry beat.

Little was it realised that within a year the Cornwall and Devon Constabularies would be amalgamated and the Cornish constable at Ladycross would be changing his helmet for a Devon & Cornwall one. As it was, the last constable stationed at the beat was Colin Trudgeon, and he left when the station closed in 1971. He was an ex-Cornwall Constabulary man, now serving as an inspector in the Devon & Cornwall Constabulary.

Most of the constables at the country beats within West Devon had a far less confusing time than the unfortunate Ladycross man, but at least he had no pubs to visit, so he did have some small blessings!

Lewdown.

Lewdown village in 1914. The police cottage can be seen on the right.

J. Spry

The original police dwelling at Lewdown, a cottage, is now known as 'Hillcrest' and is situated in the lane leading in the Lewtrenchard direction, just off the main A30. When it was being renovated recently, the bars were still *in situ* in the window of the room now used as the kitchen, which was of considerable interest as they almost certainly date back to around the time that Constable Melhuish from Lifton(7) took over as local beat officer from Constable Guscott on 1st January 1892. Another old relic of the past may be found in a little known building behind some agricultural sheds, opposite the present war memorial in the village. This, in fact, was the lock-up used on the long horse and cart journey from Bodmin court to Exeter gaol. The main road through the county ran through the village and this small building provided an overnight stop for any miscreants on their way to Exeter Prison.

The cottage first used at Lewdown was rented from the 'Squireson' of Lewtrenchard Manor, the Reverend Sabine Baring Gould. He was the local parson and squire, as well as being the author of many local books on Dartmoor and the writer of the well-known hymn 'Onward Christian Soldiers'. Having such a landlord was a bonus, for he was keen to have his local constable well looked after with respect to accommodation. Constable Copin was one of the last of the officers to occupy this cottage in the years leading up to the Great War. He went on to higher ranks in the Devon Constabulary and retired as a superintendent. It was his son,

Superintendent Francis Copin, 1943.
E. Copin

as was often the case within the force, who also became a constable and served in the late 1940s at the Ladycross beat.

By the early 1920s the old cottage at 'Hillcrest' had been given up and the station moved to the newly built county dwelling on the A30, near the crossroads by the village school. The first constable at the new station was Southwood, and he was followed, in 1928, by Uglow and then by Brewer. By 1935 Constable Bartlett was stationed at the village and it was he who was issued with a Calthorpe motorcycle, quite something in its day for a country beat station; the main road, of course, was a factor for this as well as the size of the beat. Constable Bartlett was also the first officer to move into another new (and the last) police house in 1936.

The typical Devon Constabulary square and whitewashed house stood a few yards away from its predecessor on the A30. This traditional style of the Devon police house was nicknamed a 'Major Morris' house, after the Chief Constable of the day, who had fought hard for improved conditions for his constables, especially those living in rented and unsuitable accommodation. Over a period of 20 years identical houses were built to house the rural constables. Retired officers recall that it was a great advantage living in a 'Major Morris' house – because "You knew that your curtains and carpets would always fit your next home!" These same building plans were, in fact, used time and time again.

Constable Bartlett was subsequently followed by several other officers. Constables Hosford and Alec Roper were the first, Constable Roper coming from the large 'Roper' family, whose members have graced the force for generations. Constables Brian Lee, Corbett and Sandercock followed, and then Peter Nelson occupied the beat from 1955 until 1960, when he moved to Sidmouth. He, in turn, was replaced by Frank Easterbrook, and then came another Constable Roper – David this time.

Constable Richard Norrish outside his old police house, 1993.

R. Norrish

In the September of 1962 Constable Brian Hacon took over the beat: at first he used a pedal cycle, but when the Bratton Clovelly beat closed in 1963, he switched to a motorcycle so as to be able to cover both areas. He remained until the April of 1969, when Constable Dick Norrish, the last officer, took over the beat. By the early 1970s Constable Norrish had removed to South Brent, although he returned to the area (to Okehampton station) a few years later, from where he retired in 1996.

Like many police houses, Lewdown was the base for a combined beat; it was also one of the last county beats to close in the 1970s. The closure of the stations, it should be added, was not a sudden move; they were amalgamated and enlarged as part of the process of progress. The residents of the more remote areas such as Bratton Clovelly beat could, after all, be accessed quicker by car than the former local man on his pedal cycle. Despite the understandable concerns from the pubic, the amalgamations also meant that policemen could be swifter to attend their problems and emergencies.

Lewdown, therefore, became just another old 'Major Morris' house, one of the many in the county of Devon dotted along the A30 from its borders with Dorset in the east and Cornwall in the west. This, perhaps, evokes questions from the multitude of curious holidaymakers as they journey southwards on their travels. For example, they might ask what were those curious little white houses for? If so, it is a question perhaps best answered in the words of an old retired Devon constable, when he called them "memorials to the halcyon days of policing": no more fitting description could be given to one of Major Morris's finest monuments.

Lydford.

Lydford, once the largest parish in England, was a borough in Anglo-Saxon times and a walled town of some importance. The castle was built after the Norman conquest, and in the reign of Edward I members were sent to Parliament(5). From the castle were administered Forest Laws and Stannary Laws. Although not unique, they were, in many respects, peculiar to Lydford. Prisoners languished, suffered and died in the castle dungeons and Lydford law was held in such bad repute that many grim tales have been told of it in verse and prose. The following is the first of sixteen verses written by the Tavistock poet, William Browne, in 1644:-

"I oft have heard of Lydford law,
How in the morn they hang and draw,
And sit in judgment after;
At first I wondered at it much,
But soon I found the matter such,
As it deserves no laughter."

Fortunately the upholders of the law in the modern-day police service do not have to rely upon such archaic statutes and legislation to carry out their duties.

Lydford seems to have had its fair share of strange and eventful times.

It was in the March of 1884 that Superintendent Mitchell(7) rode out to the village with Sergeant Coles and two constables to investigate a shooting. It transpired, after much deliberation, that it was at best accidental and at worst self-inflicted. A householder in a 'gentleman's residence' in the village had heard noises in his house one night. He had then loaded his shotgun and gone downstairs, only to be frightened by his own shadow. The result was that the shotgun had discharged and struck him in the face, and a lengthy police enquiry followed. The truth eventually came to light, and a very embarrassed, and wounded, 'gentleman' withdrew all complaints.

Housing constables often produced a few headaches in the days of rented police cottages, for the superintendent was required to locate accommodation for his men. In the February of 1890 the Chief Constable was informed(7) that:–

"I am hopeful of securing a cottage for a constable at Lydford junction soon, according to your wish. The other cottage mentioned is at the top of the village and is, I consider, unfit for a constable. Moreover it is owned by the village Innkeeper".

(Constable Bibbings at Lydford was being removed to Lifton because of the lease expiring on his cottage).

The superintendent was keen to keep a constable for the village, but once the house was unavailable he had to admit defeat and the village lost their officer for a while. It was, however, not long before temporary lodgings were found for an unmarried officer, and Constable Shutler took over the village beat. He, in turn, was replaced by Constable Newman of Lifton, Shutler being removed into Tavistock.

Along with Milton Abbot station, Lydford had always fallen under the control of the sergeant at Tavistock. It was not until January 1894 that Superintendent Nicholls wrote to the Chief Constable suggesting that they be transferred to the Lifton sergeant for supervision. From that date on they remained as such until their closure over 70 years later.

The cottage, later secured by Superintendent Mitchell, was situated next to the Castle Inn at Lydford, previously thought to be totally unsuitable for police purposes due to being so close to the inn. Perhaps the village constable held different views on this matter!

Various officers worked the Lydford beat. Constable Abraham was in the village at one time, along with Constable John Bastin, who came to the village in about 1903 from Milton Abbot. Constable Bazzell also appears in the records, although the only photograph of him is in his Plymouth City Police uniform as he transferred to the Devon County force when he took over the Lydford station. Constable 220 Frederick Madge spent most of the 1920s at the station with his wife, who accompanied him on his beats!

Madge was replaced, in turn, by Constables Lee, Burges and Parnell, and it was the latter, a single man, who lodged in the village with a

Above: Constable Bazzell (in the uniform of the Plymouth City Force) and family, 1910.

L. Gloyne

Below: Constable Frederick Madge 'and family' on patrol, 1925.   *Mrs M. Potts*

Lydford Special Constabulary outside Nicholls Hall, 1943, with Inspector Wiltshire, Sergeant Perryman and Constable Seldon.

Insp. R. Seldon

family called Sampson. When he married in the 1930s he moved into the newly built police house, one in the Major Morris style. His successor was Constable 279 Arthur Seldon, who was moved into the Lydford station from Bratton Clovelly. He then spent the war years from 1939 until 1945 at the Lydford beat, after which he moved to Bideford. (He did, in fact, return to the Bere Alston beat a few years later, in the 1950s). The local boys nicknamed Constable Seldon "Roughy" for reasons best known to themselves, but looking at his photograph taken outside the Nicholls Hall might give a few clues!

Following Constable Seldon's departure, Constable Ken Salter took over the beat. He, in turn, was replaced by Ken Northey, who had been at Tavistock in the late 1940s and was destined to stay at Lydford from 1953 until 1956. At that time Superintendent Jewell was in charge of the 'H' division from Crownhill and would make points with the rural men. Of course, the constables did not know when he would turn up at their points but always made sure that they were there for, having once been a sergeant at Crownhill, Jewell was held in awe by many of the men of the day.

The officer at Lifton in charge of the Lydford beat was Sergeant Perryman, who preferred to call at his stations in the early hours of the morning to deliver his constables' pay packets, as Constable Northey recalls! It was Constable Northey who cycled out to the Fox and Hounds public house to keep a point with Constable Dennis Walters from the Bridestowe beat. The Willsworthy army camp point was another: here he met the Mary Tavy officer, Constable Chapman, and sometimes, the sergeant, who could be at any of his regular stops on his beat.

Once anyone had escaped from Dartmoor Prison, the Lydford constable cycled down to Brentor railway station in order to guard the line in case the prisoner made his way on foot along it. In fact, it was not unknown for escaped prisoners to be recaptured hereabouts and to be subsequently handcuffed to Lydford police house kitchen table prior to being escorted back to the prison – a policeman's wife of those times certainly took on far more than her wedding vows might have demanded!

Ken Northey's successor at the village was Constable Willis, and he, in turn, was replaced by Constable Roberts. Being fairly quiet, however, the Lydford station was naturally one of the early ones to suffer the fate of closure. In fact, by 1966 Lydford had lost its constable, his area being amalgamated with the Mary Tavy beat and taken over by Constable Catterall (he had moved out from Bere Alston), using a motorcycle.

Milton Abbot.

In a similar vein to the slightly chequered history of the parish constables at Milton Abbot village, the Devon Constabulary officer of

1877 suffered the same unfortunate attention for all the wrong reasons. As Superintendent Cornwall reported(7) to the Chief Constable in the September of that year:–

"Sir

I have the honour to report for your information that Second Class Constable No.4 John Deacon, stationed at Milton Abbot was taken into custody and locked up at 8pm last night for being drunk and disorderly in the highway. He is also charged with a violent and brutal assault upon Mr and Mrs Blatchford, building contractor, in the town. The assault was committed in Mr Blatchford's house. He will be brought before the Magistrates tomorrow at 11am.

I have the honour to be

Sir

Your obedient servant

W.H.G. Cornwall

Supt."

The following day the superintendent reported to the Chief Constable(7) that "Deacon had appeared before the court and received fines totalling six pounds, nine shillings and fourpence, or, committed to thirteen weeks' hard labour in default". One can only assume that an example was being made of an 'upholder of the law', who had transgressed it. Whatever, Constable Deacon was replaced by Constable Cardew, who seemed to revive the local confidence in the Devon Constabulary and stayed for a few years. The police house at this time was situated up the small lane opposite the churchyard and was a dwelling that had once been used as a slaughterhouse: it was behind what was to become the site for the last police cottage in the village.

It was two years later, on 18th January 1879, that Constable Cardew was dealing(7) with an attempted murder by one Henry Hoare, a tailor and son of the local innkeeper. He had shot a local girl named Mary Peardon, then turned the revolver on himself. The doctor reported that it was unlikely that either would survive, but Cardew was instructed to sit with the injured man, Hoare, until, as expected, he died that night. Mary, fortunately, recovered from her wounds. Perhaps for Hoare the outcome was a better alternative than the possibility of having to face the hangman's noose!

It was in the November of that same year when the local shoemaker, John Martin, cut his wife's throat and then his own. Here, again, the outcome was much the same, for the man died of his injuries a few weeks later whereas his wife survived. But, surely, Constable Cardew would have been justified in wondering what sort of a village he was policing!

Cardew was eventually replaced by Constable Lang, who, in turn, was removed to Tavistock, much to his wife's protestations. She tried desperately to have her husband's removal order revoked – to no avail. "Lang", the superintendent wrote(7), "was a powerful man who would suit Tavistock and is keen to get on in the service". The result was that Lang was replaced in 1895 by a young Constable Bastin from Lifton, who had just married and was in need of a cottage. In the meantime, Milton Abbot station, along with Lydford, had transferred to the jurisdiction of the Lifton sergeant in January of the previous year, and there it was to remain until the closure of the station almost 90 years later.

By the end of the 19th century Constable John Bastin was still stationed in the village. His rented house was situated in the lane known at that time as Higher Lane, beside the local public house. Like many of his colleagues of the time, he was the holder of the St. John First Aid badge, which was worn on the right sleeve above the elbow. The

St. John Ambulance Association.

This is to certify that *P.C. John Bastin*

a certificated pupil, was Re-examined for the first

time in the month of *December* 189 8 , at

Lew Down and satisfied the Examiner.

Wm. H. Dawe

Local Hon. Secretary.

Constable Bastin's First Aid certificate, 1898.

Mrs J. Bastin

constables were tested locally and were, in their day, often the first port of call for injured persons.

Constable Bastin was eventually removed to Lydford in about 1903. He then rose through the ranks to sergeant at Torrington and retired as inspector at Exmouth in 1922. It was Constable Bastin's youngest son who became the headmaster of the Dolvin Road School in Tavistock some years later. Constable 269 Thomas Trigger was to replace John Bastin and take over his cottage with its familiar 'Devon Constabulary' sign above the door. Trigger remained for only a short time and was

Sergeant John Bastin, 1911.

Mrs J. Bastin

posted to the Mary Tavy beat in about 1904. After its rather turbulent start, Milton Abbot beat carried on quietly for the remaining decades through the war years. Constable Frank Quest appeared at the village in the last months of 1940.

Throughout the research of the history of the beat, one story was repeated time and time again. It related to a constable struck by lightning in the area. A whole generation of village people had been brought up on this childhood story, and it had embedded itself into the history of the area. Perhaps for the first time the real truth of the matter might be revealed. The constable in question had, in fact, been smoking a cigarette whilst on his cycle, a disciplinary offence of mammoth proportions. It is true that a storm had been raging that day, but the lightning strike was, in fact, an excuse for an embarrassing accident. The constable had, unfortunately, dropped the lighted cigarette down his open tunic and it had badly burned his shirt and his chest. Upon making a point with his sergeant, he was asked about the injury. Not wishing to

Constable Thomas Trigger, 1891.

G. Trigger

admit to smoking whilst riding his bike, he stated that he had been struck by lightning, but had fortunately survived his ordeal, gallantly staying on duty! Whether the sergeant swallowed this story is not known, but it seemed that the local populace did and it has now become a part of the village history.

By the 1930s the Devon Constabulary was undertaking a building programme of new dwellings for its village constables. The familiar square, whitewashed houses became landmarks in villages all over the county. Milton Abbot was also destined for one of these new 'Major Morris' houses. Unfortunately, though, these plans did not meet with the approval of His Grace the Duke of Bedford. His 'model' village of Milton Abbot, with many of the buildings being constructed for his estate workers, could not tolerate such a monstrosity, it was decided. A compromise had to be found, and a cottage, known until recently as 'Coppers Nest', opposite the churchyard, was constructed to the duke's specification. The only feature retained at the request of the Chief

Constable Trigger outside his police cottage, 1900.
G. Trigger

Constable was the small square window above the front door, a tradition of the Devon Constabulary. His Grace had won the day, and kept his village constable into the bargain.

Constable George Clayton replaced Roger Perry and was stationed in the house in the early 1950s, followed by Constable Jock Sutherland, who was eventually replaced by Constable 14 Bill Badcock in 1953. He remained 11 years until being replaced in 1964, when he moved a little distance to the new station at Lifton. The last constable at Milton Abbot was Graham Bulford: he stayed in the village until the year when many of the rural stations closed, 1970, after which he rose to the rank of Chief Inspector at force headquarters.

From a rocky start, the policing of Milton Abbot by a resident constable ended on a much happier note — it is now covered from the Tavistock station by the popular community constable, Michael Thompson, in his police car.

Constable Graham Bulford outside his police house, 1970.

Ch/Insp G. Bulford

North Petherwin.

The police station in this small village was a remote outpost of the Devon Constabulary, situated at the end of a small piece of land which jutted out into Cornwall for a few miles. It was at the sessions of the new police committee on 5th January 1858(5) when it was resolved that the two parishes of North Petherwin and Werrington ought to transfer to the Cornwall Constabulary for the purposes of policing. For some unexplained reason, however, they did not and, instead, remained under the jurisdiction of the Devon Constabulary constable, who was stationed in a cottage near the crossroads at Petherwin Gate. It was not a constabulary-owned cottage, but one rented from the Tippet family of The Barton.

The Cornwall Constabulary constable at Egloskerry was a neighbour

North Petherwin police house at Petherwin Gate, c1912.

D. Vigers

of the Devon man at North Petherwin, being stationed only a couple of miles from him. The superintendent at Tavistock, however, was some miles march away, as indeed was the sergeant at Lifton, in whose section the village was. Whilst regularly making points with the Lifton sergeant, the North Petherwin officer also had another point to keep. This one was a conference point with the Cornwall constable from Egloskerry, down at Yeolmbridge at their border on the river. Such conference points were essential for information from neighbouring beats to be passed on. The Cornish constable, Prynne, of Egloskerry is one such officer who would have been more a familiar face to the North Petherwin man than many of his own Devon Constabulary colleagues. Despite the differences in their uniforms, they were, at heart, still policemen.

Little is formally recorded about the early years of the policing of the village, although a Constable Clements had been at North Petherwin just after the turn of the century. He had clearly made an impression on his community, because when he left in 1922 the village presented him with a certificate and gift as a token of their regard for the "cordial and kindly" way in which he had performed his duties. Those duties had, in his time in the village, included 'strike duty' at Treviscoe Mine, near St. Austell. In the great industrial unrest in the clay mines in Cornwall before the Great War, many Devon constables had been drafted in to support their Cornish colleagues. Constable Clements was one such officer tasked with "quelling the militants". A photograph exists of him, taken at Treviscoe with other hardened men, who had seen some terrible fighting. The play "Stocker's Copper" was based upon those strikes and the unrest that Constable Clements witnessed first hand.

Constable Clements was later replaced by Constable Gaf, who did not stay long, for in 1924 Constable Kelly and his family arrived from Exeter to take over the beat.

By the mid-1930s a new police house had been built a few miles away at Ladycross, which resulted in the North Petherwin cottage being returned to the Tippet family and the village losing their constable. After that the area was served by the officer stationed at Ladycross, in the Werrington parish, and the only evidence left to indicate that a police house had been in the village is a faded photograph: this clearly shows the distinctive shape of the 'Devon Constabulary' arched sign above the door of the cottage now known as 'Brockings', at Petherwin Gate.

Chapter 10

THE YELVERTON SECTION

Yelverton Station.

At the time of the formation of the Devon Constabulary in 1856, Yelverton would hardly have been recognisable as a village, most of the buildings having been constructed in the last hundred years or so. Consequently, it comes as no real surprise to find that, originally, only one constable of the Devon Constabulary was stationed in the area, which, at that time, came under the 'H' division at Stonehouse as opposed to the Tavistock 'K' division. The sergeant here was stationed at Roborough, where the quarter sessions courtroom was situated, but then, when Stonehouse was taken into the Plymouth City Police area and the divisional headquarters was moved to Crownhill village, he, too, was transferred to Crownhill. Later, in 1928, the sergeant for Yelverton was also provided with a new house, which can still be seen in Tavistock Road at Crownhill, where the two distinctive Devon Constabulary dwellings are situated.

The first station at Yelverton was really just the front room of the constable's house in Moor View (a terrace off Meavy Lane). Later, when Walkhampton station closed, the constable post was transferred to Yelverton and a second officer arrived to supplement the lone constable. Usually this second constable was a single man, and it was the duty of the married constable to provide lodgings for the young officer, sometimes in his own house!

Constable Paddy Bretell, later to become an inspector at Tavistock, recalls well his time in 1936, when he was posted to lodge with the Yelverton constable and his wife. When Paddy married he was moved to Mary Tavy to take over the married beat station there. Another such single constable was Jimmy Green. He stayed a bachelor for many years, and when he left Yelverton to go to Bridestowe he again moved into lodgings in the village.

In 1950 Crownhill was taken over by Plymouth City Police and the sergeant for Yelverton moved into the old house at Moor View. At the same time, the constables were removed and placed into rented accommodation: the single constable at that time took lodgings at Glen

View in Meavy Lane, and this was to remain police lodgings for many years to follow. Meanwhile, one of the first sergeants to occupy the old house in Yelverton was Frank Burrows, the son-in-law of the last constable of Bere Ferrers. Not only through the history of the Devon Constabulary did son follow father, but it was often the case that younger constables married daughters of colleagues.

Sergeants Thomas and Burrows with Constable Battershill of Princetown, c1950.

Mrs G. Lugg

Eventually, it was decided that the old house in Moor View had become too inconvenient for a modern police station, and by 1964 a new station had been built in Tavistock Road, Yelverton. This grand, new building, with two police houses attached, was opened by the chairman of the police authority and the Chief Constable of the day, Colonel Bacon. The sergeant subsequently lived in one of the houses, with a constable in the other, while single men were lodged out with various families in the area.

With the onset of progress, a motorcycle was stationed at Yelverton, soon to be followed by a police car. Prior to this, the only motor transport had been the sergeant's own car. Much of the police work of the day was preoccupied with livestock and petty crime. It was, however, on Friday 20th February 1959 that an entry in the charge book

Opening Day at Yelverton, 1964.

Author's collection

of Yelverton station recorded thus:– "On the 14th February 1959 in the parish of Walkhampton in the County of Devon (Frank Matthews) did kill and murder Winifred Mary Matthews". Superintendent Roper of Crownhill accepted the charge that Frank Matthews had run over and murdered his wife.

The last supervisor to authorise a charge in the Yelverton charge book was Detective Sergeant E.J.E. Stowers of Plympton station. It was he who later became chief of police on the Cayman Islands and whose policeman son was promoted to be the divisional commander of 'J' division at Totnes. Divisional boundary changes took place in the mid-1960s and for a short while Tavistock and Yelverton were in separate divisions: Yelverton was transferred to the new 'G' division at Plympton, while Tavistock went into the Okehampton 'B' division, where it remained, briefly, before being returned to Plympton division. The sergeant at Yelverton had the responsibility for several stations, including Horrabridge and Roborough, but Princetown always fell under the jurisdiction of the Tavistock sergeant.

The Yelverton section area met Tavistock at Magpie Bridge in the north, while in the south, Cadover Bridge was the boundary with the Plympton sergeant's area. When the stations at Roborough and

137

Horrabridge closed, their constables were removed to Yelverton and given a car to patrol in. Yelverton, therefore, then had a sergeant and four constables. However, there was never any enquiry clerk there, the office being manned either by the sergeant or by a constable. Members of the Special Constabulary also assisted in covering the enquiry office for the public. One such special constable was William Knott of Dousland. He was a porter on the Princetown railway in his full-time occupation and a special constable in his spare time.

The last of the sergeants at Yelverton was Sergeant John Bickley, who was posted into Tavistock in 1971 when it was decided that the sergeants at both Yelverton and Lifton should move into the Tavistock sub-division. Consequently Yelverton, as had been the case so many years previously, was again without a sergeant. Nevertheless, it was still to continue as a constable station, and, eventually, the shifts carried out by the constables at Yelverton were a 9am to 5pm and a 5pm to 1am duty. A constable in a car could, therefore, be available for 16 hours a day: the night time was covered by the night duty constables at Tavistock.

Constable Gerry Falvey, 1981.
Tavistock Times

In all, three officers were left stationed at Yelverton to cover the area, along with the fourth constable as the community man for Yelverton and Horrabridge villages. Constable Gerry Falvey later became the community man for the area on his cycle, and he remained for many years in the post.

Eventually, the police station at Yelverton became too big a building for the four constables so, in 1994, a 'new' building, a former shop, in Dousland Road was bought by the police authority in order to alleviate the problem. However, the use of this 'new' building was to be short-lived for, on 1st April the following year, Yelverton was to lose its police station in the interests of economy and service. The four officers were then removed to Tavistock, these being Constables Pearce, Hartigan, Livingstone and Falvey, who still patrol the area by car.

The last few days of Yelverton station, 1994.

Author's collection

Horrabridge.

In Superintendent Mitchell's day, most of Horrabridge was in the Tavistock 'K' division area, the River Walkham being the boundary between the Tavistock and Stonehouse 'H' divisions. On 26th November 1878, Superintendent Mitchell and Constable Jones of Horrabridge were at the local railway station when a fatal accident occurred(7). This accident was within the 'H' division and Constable Jones was sent on to Stonehouse to report the matter. It was the same Constable Jones who was stationed at the village for some years. On the Christmas Eve of 1886 the superintendent's correspondence book(7) records that Jones was stabbed by a person named 'Martin' of Horrabridge. The wound was not life threatening, but the constable was confined to his bed for some days. His cottage in the village was in the street now known as Walkham Terrace, at number 2. (Some years previously the police house had been situated in the small row of cottages backing onto the river opposite the Leaping Salmon public house, long since demolished). Despite this attack, Constable Jones remained at Horrabridge until he exchanged stations with Constable Bright of Morwellham in the February of 1889. The police house remained at Walkham Terrace until after the Great War, when a new dwelling was purchased in 1919 at West Park, a terrace in the road leading to Whitchurch. This cottage had been built in 1890 and had, until then, been used by the local authority from whom it was bought for £440. It remained in the possession of the police until the closure of the station in 1968, when it was again transferred into the ownership of the Tavistock Rural District Council, this time for the sum of £2,250.

The beat book(12) of the Horrabridge station lists the constables of the area and makes interesting reading in seeing how far they were posted. In November 1923 Constable 260 Archibald Harding arrived from Noss Mayo and stayed 10 years until 1933, when he was removed to Elburton. He was replaced by Constable 331 William Martin, who was moved to the village from Bratton Flemming. He stayed 7 years, until 1940, and was removed to Alphington, near Exeter, to be replaced by Constable 325 Alec Roper. Constable Roper had been at Lewdown when he was posted to Horrabridge, only staying until 1941, when he swapped with the Tamerton Foliot constable, number 371 – Edward Parnell. Constable Parnell only stayed 3 years and, around the time that he went to Newton Ferrers, in 1944, the beat book records that most of the incidents at Horrabridge involved either road accidents or sheep being killed. Certainly a constable stationed at Horrabridge would have been an expert in these matters when he left the beat.

Constable 247 Archibald Fry arrived from Ermington to replace Parnell. Fry stayed for 8 years and even then he was only moved to Yelverton to become the local sergeant: perhaps his time at Horrabridge during the war years held him in good stead, for he hadn't had an easy time of it. On the evening of June 7th 1944 he had been called to a large disturbance at a local dance. American servicemen had been involved in a fight with locals, which had resulted in the guard being turned out

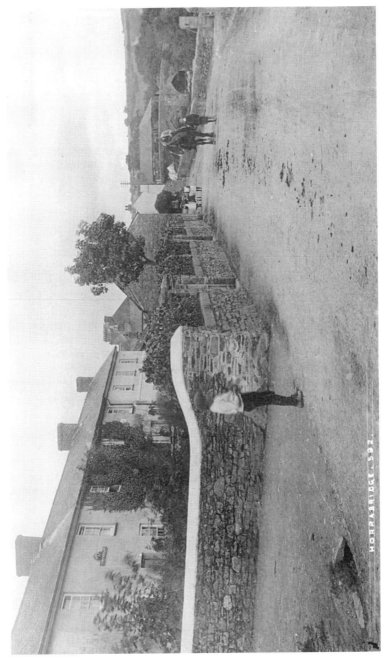

Horrabridge police house in Walkham Terrace, 1914. *C. White*

141

from the nearby camp and marching the men back to barracks. The U.S. servicemen had proved a great deal of trouble to Constable Fry. Several shop windows in Horrabridge had suffered as a result of their excessive drinking, and invariably the U.S. services had paid the bill in order to keep things quiet in the village.

Constable 427 Bert Bridge, a man who had originally joined the Lancashire Constabulary, stayed for about 12 months after Fry left and he, in turn, was replaced by Constable 91 Ken Cowman in the October of 1953. The unlucky Constable Cowman was one of the first constables of the area to have to deal with a road accident involving a police car(12). Motor Patrol Sergeant Harry Willcocks of Tavistock had swerved to avoid a horse in the main road at Horrabridge and had damaged his patrol car, almost a 'hanging offence' for a policeman in those days! Again, when Cowman left the beat in 1955, he was only moved locally to Princetown. His replacement was Charles Davies, Constable 362, who had been at Yelverton for 2 years before arriving at Horrabridge. He left to go to Bideford, and "Max" Faulkner, Constable 588, arrived from the Ashwater beat to stay a few years until Constable 198 Chris Tree, the last of the Horrabridge constables, arrived in the mid-1960s. He stayed until the closure of the station in 1968, when the constable position was transferred to the newly opened station at Yelverton.

Yelverton station remained in the Crownhill 'H' division, and then in the Plympton 'G' division, when Tavistock transferred up to the Okehampton division in the mid-1960s, and it was only later, near the time that the Devon and Cornwall forces amalgamated, that both Yelverton and Tavistock were reunited into the same Tavistock sub-division again. There Horrabridge remained, and to this day it is covered from Tavistock station. The community constable for the village is shared with the Yelverton area, but, instead of a pedal cycle, a police car is provided. The former police house in West Park, however, is still blessed with a police uniform hanging in the hall, although it is that of the present occupant – a Ministry of Defence officer, who bought the house some years ago.

Roborough.

The sessions of the police committee(5) of 5th January 1858 ordered that "A Petty Sessions room and Police Station" should be provided at "Jump". The village of Jump is now known as Roborough. Almost a suburb of Plymouth today, but in its day it was well outside the city boundaries.

Originally, Roborough was situated in the 'H' (Stonehouse) division and boasted accommodation for two constables. It was later decided, however, that the village warranted a sergeant, so one constable was removed and replaced with the sergeant. This supervisor was

The old Roborough police station and court house, 1994.

responsible for the beat constables at Yelverton, Walkhampton, Tamerton Foliot, Eggbuckland and Honicknowle, all villages in their day, as well as the constable at Jump. One of the earliest officers at Jump was Constable John Clinnick, whose grand-daughter still lives in the village. He is buried in the churchyard at Bickleigh, in which parish Roborough is situated. The sergeant, meanwhile, did not stay long at Jump. When the divisional headquarters of the 'H' division moved from Stonehouse to Crownhill village, the sergeant also moved to Crownhill.

With the advent of the motor patrol department in the 1930s, Roborough was identified as a traffic station so, therefore, it had a dual role: the local constable used the station as his beat office and the two motor patrol officers used it as their base to cover the West Devon area.

Between the two police houses was situated the petty sessions room or magistrates court, as it would now be known. The magistrates' washing and toilet facilities were shared with the police houses, so baths and washing of the constable's children were forbidden whilst the court was in session. Retired officers from the station, however, report some advantages. The court was held only on Mondays and Tuesdays each week, so for five days the courtroom was an excellent playroom for their children and for birthday parties. The court ceased functioning in the 1930s prior to the war. Even so, the conditions in the houses were not

Constable John Clinnick, c1895.

Miss J. Clinnick

particularly comfortable. One constable's wife insisted on wearing wellington boots to cook in the kitchen ever since she caught a rat rolling a potato across the floor!

Various officers were stationed at Roborough in its time, both as the local beat man and as motor patrol constables. With only two houses available, the third officer was always a single man in lodgings in the village, Constable Jack Lee being one. It was Constable Lee who eventually married his landlady's daughter. Amongst other names, such as Constables Abraham, Barnicoat, Phillips and Thomas, perhaps the best known was Constable 76 Sid Pollard. It was Sid who stayed for 17 years from 1936 to 1952. He came to the village as the beat cyclist from Tavistock, where he had been stationed since 1932. He left Roborough to finish his service in 1957 at Torquay, retiring to become a guide at Kents Cavern.

Constable Sid Pollard, 1926.

Mrs J. Southgate

Constable Jack Lee, 1936.

Mrs J. Lee

A road accident at Roborough, with Constable Sid Pollard in charge, 1940.

Mrs J. Southgate

Other officers, such as Gordon Priddell and Stanley Ball, also served at the village. During the war years a great night-time exodus of Plymouth residents came to sleep in safety on Roborough Down. A bureaucratic decision to sleep people in neat rows of cars, caravans and tents ended in tragedy when a German fighter plane found the straight lines an easy target. It was Constable Pollard who fought the case to return to hap-hazard sleeping arrangements on the Down, thus saving many lives. The war years and blitz of Plymouth also meant that Roborough, well out of the dangers of the city lights, was a safe place to store valuable documents. The two cells in the courtroom were little used for prisoners, so a solicitor in the city used one of them to store confidential papers. During this time the Tamerton Foliot beat was covered by their local officer, Constable Hansford. Once the Tamerton beat closed, however, it transferred into the Roborough area, and the two villages were covered on cycle by the Roborough man.

Eventually, the sergeant at Crownhill moved to Yelverton, and Roborough was supervised from the north. The beat man at Roborough was obliged to make points with his sergeant at the A.A. Box on Roborough Down, as well as covering the Shaugh Prior village. Beatland Cross, above Shaugh Prior, was the boundary of the Roborough beat with the Cornwood village beat. This lonely, windswept junction provided a conference point for the two constables.

The nearby Royal Marine barracks at Bickleigh provided much work for the Roborough constable, as the Yelverton station charge book bears witness. The quantity of stolen cars found dumped at the village after nights out in Plymouth was incredible! Occasionally the village constable was unfortunate enough to locate such a vehicle being driven its last few hundred yards towards the barrack gates, necessitating that month's arrest!

Constable Bill Ridgeway was stationed at Roborough in 1956 (later to retire as chief superintendent at headquarters). He recalls cycling down to Tamerton through the Plymouth City force area in order to reach the remote parts of his beat. On one such visit he was given a present of a hyacinth in a pot. Such a cumbersome load precluded him being able to cycle home, so he was obliged to push his bicycle up the hill and out of the village. He then crossed through the small section of the Plymouth City Police area, only to encounter the local city inspector from Crownhill. Had it been a Devon Constabulary inspector, questions about the large potted plant balanced on the saddle would, no doubt, have been asked. It was, however, "quite reasonable", the inspector thought, for a Devon Constabulary man to be acting in such a manner, as all 'county beat' men did!

Constable 672 Ken Harris was the last of the beat men stationed at Roborough. His spell at the station lasted from April 1964 until 1966, when the doors finally closed in preparation of the amalgamation of the Plymouth City Police force with the rest of Devon County. Once the amalgamation had occurred, Roborough village was eventually taken into the Plymouth division, but the nearby village of Bickleigh remained under the Yelverton station until the mid-1970s. However, that village, too, succumbed to the obvious and logical change to be subsequently covered by Crownhill, in Plymouth.

Roborough village had been an outpost of the West Devon area, for the constable had had his southern boundary with the city men of Plymouth, as well as having had some large and influential estates on his patch. Perhaps it was this fact that had ensured the existence of the village constable there for so long.

Walkhampton.

Walkhampton station, like Morwellham and Chillaton, was an early casualty of progress and change, surviving little more than 60 years after the formation of the Devon Constabulary. The account(15) written in a short booklet entitled *Walkhampton – Church, Parish and Village* by L. Govier, published in 1984, gives an excellent record of the policing of the area.

The earliest recorded bailiff is in the Walkhampton Manor Court Rolls for 1563 – 1585, but like many of the villages of the area the Poor Law Act of 1601 had a profound effect. Constables were appointed by the court at Jump, now known as Roborough. In 1641 John Dunning and Roger Attwill held this office. Village and court records detail Constable Peter Reed as being at Walkhampton in 1821 as the unpaid official. By 1847, only 9 years before the formation of the Devon Constabulary, there were four such officers of the parish holding the title of constable – Messrs. William Gosling of Knowle, Samuel Hannaford of Easter Green, John Giles of Lowery Steant and John Creber of Horseyatt.

It was not until 1861, some 5 years into the era of the Devon Constabulary, that the school records for the village provide any information in respect of the children of the local constabulary. It is then stated that Richard Howe, constable of Walkhampton, had his daughter admitted to the school. Again, 2 years later, Constable Samuel Seabright's daughter is shown to have attended. Constables Constantine Bowman and William Greek followed in 1864 and 1871 respectively. It is worthy of note, however, that unpaid parish officers continued to be appointed until 1872: James Maddock, local blacksmith, was the last to hold the parish position as a forerunner to the modern-day special constable.

The names recorded by L. Govier as constables for the village are Border (1882–7), Dymond (1892–7), Hurford (1897–8), Hart (1900), Fry (1902), Clogg and Podger (1906), West (1914–8) and another Constable West, who left in the early 1920s to supplement the single officer at Yelverton. And so came the end of an era, one in which Walkhampton, being a major parish on the western side of Dartmoor, had warranted a resident constable for many years.

The dwelling rented by the Devon Constabulary as the local police cottage was Staddon Heights. This is a building opposite the site of the former post office, near the village school, much altered now, but still standing in silent witness to many of the village events of yesteryear.

❋ ❋ ❋ ❋ ❋

Chapter 11

A MOBILE POLICE FORCE

(The Motor Patrol Department)

By the beginning of the century the motor car was coming to be regarded as a menace. The Motor Car Act of 1903, nevertheless, did away with the need for a red flag to be carried at the front of a motor vehicle as had hitherto been the case. In its place it imposed a general 20mph speed limit but, as one would expect, people were not content with sticking to the limit! The police were therefore used to trap these speeding offenders with stopwatches. The *Devon and Exeter Gazette* of 19th September 1905 states:–

"Captain Gordon, Superintendent of Police for Tavistock and Lifton, has successfully prosecuted a number of persons for driving motor cars at excessive speeds. His first case was at Lifton, where the defendant was charged with negligence as well as driving at an excessive speed, and was fined, with costs £23. The other day he instituted another prosecution at Lifton for driving at an excessive speed but the Magistrates dismissed the case. The chairman said that the car was not very much going over the legal limit and the bench were not at all satisfied with the accuracy of the constable's watches. They asked the superintendent to represent to the Chief Constable that stop watches ought to be provided by the county."

As a result of this matter raised from Tavistock, the Chief Constable issued this somewhat complicated instruction to superintendents:–

"An ideal trap is a measured distance of at least 400 yds. A to A, a man at each end to signal the passing his point, B a uniform man further on to stop by signal offending cars, and two men handling one tested stop watch in unison, these two being in such a position as enables them to see A—A and B and to signal to B if necessary – two men at one watch are much less open to criticism than two watches."

(It is not known what effect this order had on the prosecution cases for speeding cars. Its very nature probably drove the officers to find something less involved to deal with!)

With the increasing use of motor transport, the police had naturally to move with the times also. It was, however, many years before Tavistock station was to have its own police cars, even though a new department was created in the Devon Constabulary – the motor patrol department. In its day, being on motor patrol really must have been quite something.

The first traffic car in the West Devon area was stationed at Roborough, not at Tavistock. The reason behind this was because of the increased use of vehicles by the Plymouth city travelling criminal. There was also the problem of speeding cars going across Roborough Down, which needed dealing with. And so the Roborough station became West Devon's first traffic station, with two constables crewing the vehicle: Motor Patrol Constable Jack Lee, an unmarried officer who lodged in the village, was the partner of Constable Clifford Phillips. They used a Ford Popular patrol car. Constable Sid Pollard was also stationed at Roborough, but was the beat man with a cycle.

When Constable Phillips left Roborough, he was replaced on the motor patrol by Sid Pollard. A few years earlier Sid had been run down by a stolen lorry at Shaugh Prior, which had left him with a badly injured leg. Consequently, he welcomed the change to traffic patrol and was to remain at Roborough for another 17 years! Constable Pollard's daughter still recalls that the vehicle her father used on patrol was an Austin with the registration number FDV 419, which was garaged at the rear of the station.

The motor patrol officer's house, which Constable Phillips vacated, was not reallocated to another traffic officer. It was, instead, used to house the wife and family of a Constable Bob Southcott of the Devon force, while he was temporarily serving with the military in post-war Germany: sadly, he never returned, losing his life out there. It was also at this time that the motor patrol sergeant in charge of the Roborough traffic car was stationed at Plympton. There he had his own crew of constables in addition to the Roborough crew, who would travel hundreds of miles a week covering the southern and western areas of Devon. They even travelled so far as Dartmouth on a night shift, still making points at police stations as in those days they were not equipped with radios. Added to this, the officers of the day had to wear distinctive, but very uncomfortable, uniforms according to the pensioners of the Devon Constabulary's traffic department. They recall that it included flat caps and breeches with long leather gaiters up to the knees.

When the Plymouth City Police took over Crownhill village a few years after the Second World War, the motor patrol crew moved from Roborough and retreated out into the county to Tavistock, thus leaving behind them the solitary beat constable at Roborough with his cycle. There, the two traffic officers were allocated the police houses at Drake Villas, near Drake's statue, while their car was lodged in a garage at the rear of The Bedford Hotel. However, despite now being based at Tavistock, the motor patrol officers were directly supervised by the Plympton traffic sergeant and worked independently of the local Tavistock station officers, travelling, like their Roborough predecessors, many miles throughout Devon.

As time inevitably marched on, so came changes and, eventually, two

Above: Motor Patrol Constables Ken Northey and Bill Bowen, 1958.

K. Northey

Below: A Triumph Vitesse patrol car, near Lydford, 1966.

B. Phillips

151

new houses (now in the grounds of St Peter's School) at Greenlands estate were built by the county for the two traffic constables – then Motor Patrol Constables Northey (formerly of the old Lydford beat some years before) and Graham Holloway. A new garage was also built – next to the dwellings – for the motor patrol car, and the two officers then operated their mobile patrols from the Greenlands houses.

Another significant change, in line with the technological advances of the age, was the installation of an in-car radio. Initially, the Devon motor patrol crews shared a Plymouth City Police radio on the city frequencies. Nevertheless, it was most effective: if Tavistock police station needed the motor patrol, all that was needed was a telephone call to the Plymouth City force headquarters at Greenbank, from where a call would then be put out over the radio. It was regarded as an incredible advance.

By 1958 Constable Northey had been joined by Motor Patrol Constable Bill Bowen and, as before, their duties included attending all serious accidents and incidents, being supported, if necessary, by their beat colleagues. This, then, continued to be the pattern over the next few years, but by the mid-1960s a major reorganisation became inevitable as plans to amalgamate the Devon Constabulary with Plymouth City Police and Cornwall County Constabulary began to take shape.

It was about this period that Motor Patrol Constable Dick Hancock arrived at Tavistock, an officer who was to remain for 17 years and claim the longevity record for an officer serving in the town. Motor Patrol Sergeant "Buddy" Willcocks was the officer supervising the Tavistock crew. Now retired, Constable Graham Holloway recalls that there were two cars based in the town and, with a primary responsibility for prison escapes, both officers had telephones in their houses – quite a luxury in those days. The vehicles of his era included Triumph Vitesses, Ford Zephyrs – black in colour with a shiny chrome bell on the front! – and Austin A70 Herefords, all classics in the memories of officers long since retired.

In 1967 the Devon & Cornwall Constabulary was formed, and Tavistock was identified as being an excellent location for a new traffic department to cover the busy A30 and A38 trunk roads to the north and south of the town. As a result, new houses at Courtlands Road were built to house the increase of officers needed to man the new department. However, as soon as the houses had been built the plans changed: Okehampton, on the A30, was to have its own traffic department, which remains to this day, and Plympton, in the south, was also created as a new traffic department to cover the A38 trunk road. Nevertheless, the houses were not wasted as the older houses used by the beat officers in Tavistock were disposed of and Courtlands Road became the new police house estate for the town's policemen. The Greenlands traffic unit, too, was used for housing other beat constables, but the fact remained that Tavistock had lost its motor patrol.

A road accident at Gulworthy Cross, 1969.

P. Gibson

The traffic departments at Okehampton and Plympton still cover out to Tavistock, some 30 years later. Although still dealing with the more serious of accidents, their role has also developed. With the increased use of firearms in criminal activity, the traffic department at Plympton have regularly armed officers on patrol in the Plymouth city and West Devon area, and these are on call at a moment's notice when needed to support their beat colleagues.

And so a small chapter in the policing history of Tavistock drew to an end barely 15 years after it had started in the town. With the advance of mechanisation, progress also comes at a quicker pace, and change seems to follow all the sooner for it.

Chapter 12

VOLUNTEERS ONE AND ALL

(The Special Constabulary and War Reserves)

It might justifiably be argued that the Special Constabulary is the senior of the police services, having been introduced before the formation of the regular force in many counties. The Special Constables Act of 1831 permitted local authorities to appoint suitable men as voluntary police officers, to be paid certain allowances for their work and to be called upon in times of emergencies. Today they are a supplementary organisation to support and assist the regular force wherever they are required.

As can be seen from the Walkhampton records, once a regular Devon Constabulary constable was appointed to the village, the special constable continued in post for some time.

In 1911 the Home Secretary had issued an important circular; it urged police authorities throughout the country to recognise the importance of a continuous classified registration of suitable persons. Such persons would be available to assist the police if any serious emergency should arise. This register would afford a means of organising at least two branches of a permanent police reserve. The primary would be called the "First Police Reserve". This would be composed of police and army pensioners as well as others who might be trained to step up into the ranks of the regular police force when required. The "Second Police Reserve" would consist of special constables, classified as to whether they were to be paid or not, or just called merely to assist in moments of danger. The circular put out by the Home Secretary read:–

"Home Secretary's Circular 15th September 1911 – First Police Reserve – The "First Police Reserve" should consist of men of the most useful class, namely, men who are accustomed to discipline and have been trained in the police or army, or who are otherwise specially qualified for police work. It will probably be that the men of this class should be temporary, that is, that they should be taken into service as county or borough constables with a limited engagement. These men could wear uniform if thought desirable. The "Second Police Reserve" would consist of all those registered as willing to be sworn in as special constables. These should be classified as to whether they are paid or unpaid".

It was not really until the Great War of 1914 that the Special

Constabulary came to the fore, and remained in that position until the present day. (Tavistock and the surrounding parishes had many more special constables than regular officers). The special constable of the early to middle part of the 20th century tended to be an older man, who donned his uniform on "high days and holidays". For example, Goose Fair and the various country shows were usually policed, in the main, using the Special Constabulary. The relationship between the regular force and the specials was often tenuous in the early years, but since the 1970s the role of special constable is barely distinguishable to that of a regular officer when they are on duty. The war years of the 1940s saw the Special Constabulary and first police reserve used to great effect in West Devon: whilst regular constables were away fighting for king and country, police pensioners were brought back into service and putting on their uniforms once more, perhaps for the first time in years. Members of the first police reserve were paid officers, a hybrid between the volunteer specials and regular officers. They, in fact, wore the same uniform as the regulars, with identical powers.

War Reserve Constable Fred Connett with Constable Arthur Walters of Whitchurch and Inspector Derges of Tavistock, 1942.
D. Connett

When Constable Fred Connett of Whitchurch retired in 1938 he thought that he had seen the last of his uniform. He was, however, soon back in it, looking somewhat older than most of his colleagues when the war broke out. He was joined by several other retired constables and ex-army servicemen in the town and villages around. It was, nevertheless, Maurice Gloyne of Lifton who was the last of the first police reserve officers still to be employed in West Devon. He retired in about 1955 at a senior age and is remembered by the police pensioners as mainly being engaged on simple duties in the area, such as traffic control and foot patrols. Although he was paid, he did not carry out the same commitments as his regular colleagues.

The first police reserve system ended in the late 1950s and left just the volunteer Special Constabulary to carry on its work in supporting the regular constabulary. One such voluntary special constable was George Jones of Lewdown. His wartime exploits were kept a guarded secret for decades, and it was not until some 40 years later that his full role in the police service was ever disclosed. His day to day work was driving the milk collection lorry for the creamery at Lifton, work that took him all over West Devon as a matter of course. His presence was a natural sight in the area and needed no explanation or disguise. Little did people realise, however, that beneath his driver's seat was a sealed box used for transporting official government papers from police station to police station. Yes, he was a delivery man in every meaning of the word – with his secret role in the war effort as a special constable. Indeed, he was a trusted member of the constabulary, fulfilling a vital role for years during the hostilities.

Each village had its own compliment of special constables, each proud to be part of the organisation. Their aged members were also a great contrast to the younger officers in the Special Constabulary service of today, an aspect that was particularly noticeable in the post-war years, when the Devon Special Constabulary held training 'take-over' days. These, in fact, took place once a year and involved the specials taking over control of the whole of the constabulary for one day as a training exercise. Some special constables did not need any supplementary training, being on duty at stations more than they were off duty. One such man was the one-legged special constable who carried out enquiry office duties at Yelverton station. His one wooden leg precluded too strenuous a commitment unfortunately, but he served a useful purpose nevertheless. He was, though, rather broad in his Devon accent and this often caused a few problems! On one occasion his pronunciation of "Roborough" caused great consternation when a constable stationed at Tavistock rang Yelverton and wanted to leave a message on the "robo-phone" telephone message machine. "I want the robo-phone" he asked. The special constable, bright as a button, was aware that the police station at Roborough had no telephone as it was soon to be closed. He

Inspector Derges with Tavistock wartime special constables, 1942.

Author's collection

informed the constable that "There 'baint no phone down to "Roobra, we got it here in a box". "No, no" said the constable, "Give me the Robo-phone". "Listen", said the special, "I told you there 'baint no phone down to Roobra, so you can't have it, you deaf or zummit?" and he promptly slammed the phone down. The constable never did get to leave the duty messages on the Robo-phone!

Without doubt, the Special Constabulary came into the limelight when there was 'one away' from Dartmoor Prison (an expression used to this day to describe an escaper). Check points would often include a special constable to support their regular colleagues. Indeed, over the years a few convicts have been 'brought in' by specials! Special Sergeant Horace Smith of Tavistock had such a knack for capturing convicts. He once caught one at Tavistock North railway station, and had the pleasure of carrying out the 'right' to return him home to Princetown. It was Sergeant Smith who took part in the search for Frank 'Mad Axeman' Mitchell.

The rank structure of the Special Constabulary, until 1979, was the same as the regulars. They had constables, sergeants and inspectors, but this was altered to avoid confusion between a regular officer and a Special Constabulary officer. This change also put to bed some of the dislike of certain quarters of the regular service toward the Special Constabulary.

Many families had generations who served in the specials. One, a farming family, was the 'Palmers' of Gulworthy, whose involvement with the specials ended in the early 1990s, when John Palmer retired from the service as sub-divisional officer. He was the third generation of his family, who had served the constabulary for most of this century.

The special constables of today drive police vehicles and wear identical uniforms. They are very much an important part of the policing of West Devon, and their great advantage is that, being local officers, their knowledge of the area is immense. They are not posted to all parts of the constabulary, but serve generally in one area for their whole service. They are also still volunteers and unpaid, coming on duty when they are able to serve, and are the backbone of policing most large events of the area. With financial restrictions being placed upon forces, the Special Constabulary provides excellent and valued service at minimal cost to the public and will, no doubt, remain to do so for many years to come.

✳ ✳ ✳ ✳ ✳

Chapter 13

POLICING THE PRISON IN OUR BACKYARD

(Dartmoor Prison)

Many books have been written about Dartmoor Prison, possibly the best known of all jails. To repeat information held elsewhere would be duplication and unnecessary. However, a book about the policing of West Devon would be incomplete without some reference to it.

The significant effect that the prison had upon the policing of the area was only really felt at times of break-outs. Too numerous to mention in these few pages, but in their day they represented a massive challenge for the local police. In fact, the pride of the division rested upon the men of the Devon Constabulary to prevent the escapee from reaching anywhere outside the division: heads would positively roll should the convict be caught outside of the force area! At all costs the escapee had to be prevented from getting off the moors.

The prison has seen mutiny, murder and even a *break-in*, but throughout that time police officers and prison warders have worked side by side for a common purpose. And the one constable stationed at Princetown was the link between the prison and the Devon Constabulary: it was beholden upon him to telegraph his seniors at Tavistock if anything was amiss.

It was Constable Cardew of Princetown who, in the August of 1890, took into custody one Joseph Denney. Denney was a coloured man, a native of Barbados, who had broken *into* Dartmoor Prison(7). Sergeant Coles rode out from Tavistock and Denney was remanded to the cells – at the Princetown police house because the Tavistock cells had recently been flooded. Incidentally, Denney eventually got his wish and was soon back behind prison bars again.

Escapes and recaptures are duly recorded in Superintendent Mitchell's correspondence book(7). One such entry of 1887 reads:-

"Nov 8th 1887
Sir,
I have the honour to report for your information that on yesterday morning shortly after nine o'clock a convict (lately convicted in the name of Frederick Scott) escaped from Dartmoor Prison, and was captured at about 2pm by Constable Kemp at Mary Tavy (in a field). The convict had been seen in the field

159

by a boy. The boy told the Constable and soon the fellow was found under a corn rick almost out of sight. Constable Kemp and Sergeant Richards took the convict to the prison at about 6 o'clock
I have the honour to be, Sir,
Your obedient servant,
Signed William Mitchell,
Supt."

The pony patrols of warders, now long since gone, were a common sight on the moors. Much earlier, but just as common, was the sight of the warders armed with rifles and sabres. Indeed, early photographs of the armed warders bear silent witness to failed break-out attempts, some of which took place outside the confines of the prison walls. In the November of 1880, for example, Superintendent Mitchell grimly announced the following, after a failed attempt by prisoners to escape from the working party at the prison quarry(7):–

"November 14th 1880
Sir,
I have the honour to report for your information that on Friday last, the 12th instant, a party of convicts working at the quarry, Princetown made an attempt to escape. One convict struck down a Warder, and a second convict struck down another warder. The two convicts (one named Thomas Bevan and the other, Thomas O'Brian) then endeavoured to get off by running out of the quarry, at the same time calling upon all the other convicts to join. But the warders and guard were prepared and three of the guard fired at the two convicts, Bevan and O'Brian. Bevan was shot dead and O'Brian was mortally wounded. One of the warders is badly wounded. The convicts were promptly marched into the prison.
I have the honour to be Sir
Your obedient servant
(Signed) William Mitchell
Superintendent."

Whenever there was a break for freedom, a well-rehearsed 'prison escape plan' was put into action involving police officers from all over the division. Check points and road blocks were set up and, despite their primitive nature without radio communications, they were surprisingly effective. In fact, most convicts were recaptured within hours, but a few did get away, one, indeed, so far as Jamaica in the West Indies!(6)

The road blocks were not routinely armed, but occasionally, depending upon the prisoner involved, a revolver was made available. Prison warders, too, doubled up with constables in these miserable of duties, which often took many hours (a situation that was to exist even up until the 1980s when, following the introduction of the police helicopter, alternative means of seeking convicts were employed). The local officers of the stations close to Tavistock sometimes fared better than those brought in from elsewhere to man the check points. Constable Connett, of the Whitchurch beat, was one. His son, later to become a local clerk in the magistrate's office, would walk out across the moors to his father with a jug of hot coffee, upon the orders of his mother.

Constable 191 Harry Rice inspecting documents at an armed prison escape checkpoint, 1932.

D. German

A prison escape checkpoint near Peakhill Farm, Dousland, Yelverton, 1926.
D. German

Constable Northey of Lydford was one of the less fortunates, however. His point was often at Moorshop crossroads between Tavistock and Princetown, a bleak place at the best of times. On one occasion, he was posted there in deep and driving snow at five o'clock on a winter's night. With just his cape and helmet for protection, he remained there until seven o'clock the following morning, when the cold became too much for him. He then withdrew to the side of the road and sat in a ditch for shelter (still keeping watch) only for his inspector to come by soon afterwards and subsequently place him on a charge for leaving his post!

Sometimes, when the weather became bad, officers were left out all day and all night without refreshment as a young Constable Jacknelle of Plympton found to his cost, when he was posted to the Cadover point. He was later recovered, suffering from the cold, on the following day, when a relief constable finally got through.

There are, of course, many other tales of hardship over and above the time when a convict once made a bid for freedom just as the staff at Tavistock station were sitting down to Christmas lunch! A former Ladycross constable, for example, recalls, on one occasion, being allowed to climb aboard a traction engine, whose driver took pity on him and stopped for a while, so that he could warm himself by the

The Chief Constable, Major Morris, with Constable Thomas Colwill preparing for a search by plane for an escaped prisoner, c1936.

Keith A. Saunders

firebox. Suffice to say, the comfort of a warm police car is a modern-day luxury by comparison!

The prison has seen numerous upsets and troubles over the decades, but none perhaps more famous than the great mutiny of 1932. It was late January that year, after discontent had been smouldering in the prison over food, that the frustration and anger of prisoners boiled over: the prison staff were attacked and buildings set alight. As a result, police officers from all over Devon had to be called in, supported by their colleagues from the Plymouth City Police force, but it was not until the Plymouth City Chief Constable, Mr Wilson, and the County Police superintendent, Mr Smith, from Crownhill, entered the prison that the riots were eventually quelled. Even then it took the presence of the new Chief Constable of Devon, Major Morris (a one time governor at the prison), before peace was properly restored.

Rebuilding took some time, as did the trials of the ringleaders and others involved. The initial hearings were held at Tavistock magistrates court, but the travelling from Princetown became difficult, so it was decided to turn Princetown town hall into a temporary courthouse. An iron dock was fabricated, and prisoners were then handcuffed to it after being marched from the nearby jail each day under heavy escort. Armed police officers were also stationed at the court.

One constable, George Roper, travelled daily in the police furniture removal lorry to Princetown from his lodgings in Newton Abbot. His

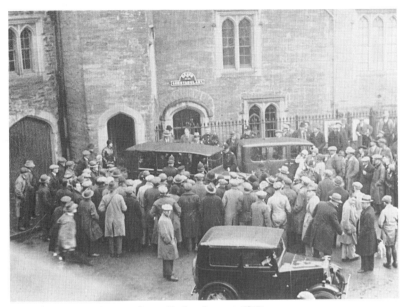

Above: Prison rioters arrive at Tavistock court, 1932.

D. German

Below: Prison rioters arrive at Princetown town hall assize court, 1932.

Ret'd Supt D. Roper

landlady at the time always gave him fried mackerel for breakfast, but he recounts that they rarely survived the journey!

A large prosecution case was put together by the police. The sergeant at Lifton, Sergeant Derges, collated much of the papers – a job that took him from his Lifton station for many weeks. Whether this mammoth task held him in good stead is not known, but he later returned to Tavistock station in the war years as the inspector.

The years between the wars were a troubled time for the police, who were responsible for policing the exterior of the prison. Because of the risks involving some of the prisoners, who were in custody due to their involvement in the Irish Republican Army, a second constable was stationed at the village from the 1920s until the start of the Second World War. This constable was a single man, who took lodgings in the village and who was used to patrol the village and the perimeter of the prison at night. Constable Charlie Battershill was the last of these single constables used for this purpose, and, although he left at the outbreak of war, he later returned as the full-time married officer in the late 1940s.

Many of the infamous London gangland criminals were held at the prison. One such man was Frank Mitchell, known by many as the 'Mad Axeman'. Stories within the police service abound in respect to Mitchell. He is reputed to have once picked up the rear of a Triumph Vitesse police car and turned it round, instructing the occupants to return to Plymouth from where they had come – but not in such polite terms. Mitchell, however, met his demise following an escape in the 1960s and was never seen again.

Other convicts made their escapes in the most imaginative of ways. On one occasion three men hijacked a delivery lorry and burst out through the gates in their bid for freedom: the lorry was severely damaged, but served its purpose. Men have also hidden in pigswill bins and have employed every possible means to effect their freedom, but few held onto it for long. Like the convict in Dickens' classic *Great Expectations*, modern-day convicts run the risks of what Dartmoor can offer. Indeed, some have died in their attempts, while many have become lost. One such unlucky escaper ran for hours in the mist across the moors only to find that when the mist lifted, he was running straight back to the prison and the open arms of the warders!

Modern-day convicts, when recaptured, often remark on how useful the huge television mast at North Hessary had been as a landmark to get away from the prison. But rarely these days do men run off very far into the depths of the moors. Huge lines of policemen and warders crossing the moors are a sight now long since gone.

It was invariably the 'unsaid right' of the officer who captured an escaped convict to have the duty of returning him to the jail. Some escapees are happy to be caught, for when they have had their freedom for 24 hours their prison debts are cleared – but along with this goes the risk of lost remission. Mixed emotions are often voiced by constables at the return of a prisoner to Princetown. When chasing your convict, a strange relationship develops. The satisfaction of a job well done in returning a man to prison is often tainted with a degree of pity; some say it's like returning a bird to its cage after a small taste of hard-fought-for freedom.

Perhaps the lasting epitaph of the involvement in prison life of the men from the constabulary should be left to 'Rubber-bones' Webb, a convict who escaped from warders at Tavistock railway station. He was at large for three days and was hunted by a body of men with Mrs Blagdon's bloodhounds (see chapter 9 – Bratton Clovelly). He was eventually caught at Meldon suffering badly from exposure, the weather being bitterly cold. When caught, he gave himself up without a struggle saying "I'm the man you're looking for". In 1954, writing in *The People* on his prison experiences, he paid tribute to the men of the Devon Constabulary:–

"After my capture things started to happen. Kind arms took hold me – the arms of the Devon Constabulary. "Poor devil" said one. "He must be nearly dead" said another. Then I found a paper bag full of cakes in one hand and an orange in the other, while a cigarette was being thrust in my mouth and someone else was lighting it. I'll never forget those grand fine Policemen. They took me to Tavistock police station and I felt like a long lost son coming home. One of them took off my shoes, bit by bit like a nurse. Another brought a bowl of warm water and began washing my feet. Yes, it really happened – a copper washed the feet of a criminal. I was a gunman, an old lag, and he washed my feet. It was too much. I am afraid the tears started in my eyes. I did not stay long in that dreamworld. Very soon two Warders arrived from Dartmoor Prison."

Chapter 14

MURDER MOST FOUL

(Murders of West Devon)

Society has never been without the shadow of man's cruelty to his fellow man; West Devon is no exception. All of the murders recorded in West Devon, however, were committed by someone known to the victim. From the days before the formation of the Devon Constabulary to the present time, the victim has always been an acquaintance of the offender.

Budgehill(11), in the parish of Whitchurch, was the scene of one of the earliest recorded murders of the area. It was here, on 16th of February 1815, that Mary Metters, the wife of the farmer at Budgehill, was struck down with a billhook by one Sam Norton, a servant. Norton was eventually arrested, brought to trial and his fate encountered publicly at the front of the gaol at Exeter, where he was hanged. The grave of Mary Metters in the parish churchyard is inscribed with the brief details of her demise. The name of her assailant was added, it seems, as an afterthought. Perhaps the hangman's rope was insufficient punishment, and a lasting humiliation of his misdeeds was needed to make amends.

In Victorian Tavistock it was easy to cry 'murder' without the modern-day forensic advances. Jane Wakeham, for example(7), a resident of the workhouse, was arrested just prior to the Christmas of 1878 for the wilful murder of her six-month old child. After being remanded in custody for two weeks, the visiting magistrate released her without charge, for no evidence was found to support the allegation.

Not so in the case of Alfred Davis of Bannawell Street in 1890(7). Tavistock town of the 19th century was a place where lodging houses abounded and poverty was rife. Housing conditions in the more run-down areas were poor, with overcrowded rooms breeding discontent amongst residents. Davis rented a room in a house in this old part of the town from an elderly lady called Jane Caser. A woman of "weak intellect", she was aged seventy-three when Davis felled her with a dining chair. He was a large and powerful man and was remanded to Plymouth Prison to face trial at Exeter. His demise is unknown, but

Superintendent Mitchell went to great pains to ensure that several police constables escorted him on the train from Tavistock to Millbay as well as to the gaol. Mitchell had resided as a neighbour of Mrs Caser and, no doubt, knew the prisoner personally.

This was the last murder of Mitchell's time, for he was to retire just prior to the well-documented incident at Peter Tavy in the November of 1892, when Emma Doidge and William Rowe were both shot a little way out of the village by a jilted suitor, one William Williams. Williams also attempted to take his own life, but failed: how ironic it is that the judicial system should end it for him some weeks later at Exeter gaol.

The detailed account by Gerry Woodcock in volume eight of his *Tavistock's Yesterdays* is an excellent account of the events. Had the police records and reports been available at the time of writing the article, no doubt it would have resulted in an entire book dedicated to the subject.

The tragic events at Peter Tavy received national publicity. Petitions were signed and thousands put their names to requests for clemency for Williams – to no avail. One of the officers involved in the investigations, Constable Callard, moved away from West Devon a few months after the case. Clearly many reports and accounts never mention the personal effect that such incidents have upon the constables who are embroiled in them. Perhaps the perception of the public is such that police officers are not affected by such tragedy, and take it on as a day to day job. Constable Callard and his successors would almost certainly disagree.

It was not only in the 19th century that such incidents were seen in the West Devon area. It was at 7.40pm on February 14th 1959 that a terrible 'accident' took place on Knowle Down, near Horrabridge(9). A lady had 'fallen' from a car, and her husband reported driving over her accidentally. At that time Constable Phillips, of Yelverton, was a local probationary officer and it was, perhaps, this case that helped him considerably in his formative years, for he was ultimately to retire from the force as an Assistant Chief Constable. Phillips was also to hold the post of being one of the sergeants to live in the police station at Tavistock. However, to revert to the 'incident', blood splatterings were later located inside the car and a lengthy investigation followed under the supervision of Detective Sergeant Jack Tarr (he came from Plympton and was to become known throughout the force in the years to follow as one of the most successful detectives ever). Constable John Hurn, renowned for his expertise at plan drawing, also attended the scene, and the eventual outcome was that Matthews was imprisoned for life for murder. One wonders how such a crime would have been solved without the intuition and sharp eyes of the 'ordinary' constable on the beat.

This chapter doesn't end there, but painful memories still fresh in the minds of those left to remember preclude the mentioning of matters of recent history. Perhaps, instead, a final thought should be given to the police officer embroiled in such tragedy not of his own making. It is, after all, to the police service that we turn in times of crises, and never more so than when a death is caused by the intent or wilful act of another. It is not just those who are so terribly involved that become touched by its consequences: behind what is imagined to be a hard and austere shell of the constable, lies someone capable of being as touched by tragedy as the next man. Perhaps the lessons learned by Constable Callard of Lamerton in leaving behind painful memories of a Peter Tavy murder should not be forgotten. The thoughts of Superintendent Mitchell, when his neighbour was struck down yards from where he, himself, lay, must be considered. Surely the constable of today, who arrives at the scene of a suspicious death, is as entitled to be as touched as anyone? The only difference is that the expectations of the public that fall upon the police are great, and their independent and unfailing professionalism must prevail throughout, until, perhaps, when the sanctuary of the police station is reached. Perhaps then, and only then, can the real effect of being a police officer involved in such tragedy be displayed, in some quiet corner, away from public scrutiny, where generations of constables have shown that sensitivity and caring is a quality to be proud of and not ashamed of.

Chapter 15

NEVER A STONE UNTURNED

(Early days of Dartmoor Rescue)

Parliament has for many years laid the responsibility of searching for missing persons onto the shoulders of the police. Never was that obligation felt so strongly than when dealing with persons missing on Dartmoor. Once described as "England's last wilderness", Dartmoor rises to over 2,000 feet above sea-level. The 20th century has brought about many changes, a significant one being the amount of time that we have to spend at leisure. This, in turn, led to rambling on Dartmoor becoming a popular pastime that increased year by year as more and more people came to enjoy the tranquillity and beauty of this unspoilt area. But, with this increase in visitors, so came an upward surge in work for the local constabulary: when someone was reported missing on the moors, it was, invariably, to the police that the public turned. However, the officers of the Devon Constabulary were poorly equipped and not trained for searching on the open moors and, instead, soldiers training in the area, as well as local farmers and other hikers, were employed to assist in their obligations to find the missing ramblers. Moreover, few policemen of the time were keen to hike over the moors – a cape and helmet was no match for the weather that Dartmoor was capable of producing. One notable exception, though, was Constable Derek Roper of Princetown. It was his police house which served as a focal point for many searches for missing persons, and it was inevitable that his influence would change the course of history in this respect.

It was not until 1968 that events were about to overtake the ability of the local police. During a severe snowstorm that year many schoolchildren were stranded on the moors, and Constable Roper used the services of the local outward-bound centre warden, Bill Ames, to assist in co-ordinating and effecting the rescue of the children. That incident was quickly followed by further events of a similar nature until, eventually, it was found that Dartmoor was in need of a group of experienced volunteers who would be willing to take on the responsibility of searching the moors for missing people, on behalf of the police. Like the many other moorland and mountainous parts of

Great Britain, Dartmoor was soon to have its own rescue team: a meeting held that year at Tavistock police station laid the foundations of the Dartmoor Rescue Group of today.

The team at Tavistock was soon to be followed by a section at Okehampton. Formed by Fred Barlow BEM, it provided a service on the higher moorland to the north. Other teams were also soon created: the outward-bound school at Holne became the Ashburton section, while another, the Plymouth section, was formed mainly from dockyard workers, who were keen hikers. One thing was constant throughout all this time – the responsibility for searching the moors remained with the local police. They used these volunteers to carry out the work on their behalf and supported their operations. Indeed, it was part of the duties of all subsequent constables stationed at the Princetown beat to become involved in such work.

A few decades later the Dartmoor Rescue Group boasts over 160 members. It continues to be called upon by the police and has developed into an efficient and well-respected rescue team. Its long and distinguished history is too significant to fully detail here, but its roots are certainly worth including in this record. Furthermore, from the formative years, in the days of Constable Roper, the Dartmoor Rescue Group has never yet turned down a call from the police for assistance – long may that continue!

Chapter 16

THE CURRENT SCENE

(West Devon policing in the 1990s)

It is inevitable that change will take place in society, and it is necessary for the police service to meet that change and adapt to it. Without doubt, in the eyes of the general public, one of the most significant changes has been the closure of the small rural stations and police houses. It is, of course, proper that the public have the right to demand a speedy and efficient service from the police and, unfortunately, the old system of police houses was not always the quickest way of reacting to the demands of society. Hence many were amalgamated and constables were left covering larger beats with a car and radio. 'Unit beat policing'

The modern 'unit beat policeman', 1967.
Devon & Cornwall Constabulary

was the modern term for this system, which was gradually introduced in the 1960s and early 1970s, when many police houses were closed and officers were centralised into stations. However, it was not entirely new as Chillaton and Walkhampton, for example, were closed in the 1920s.

So, although we might like to think of change as being a new concept, it is not always the case. The police service is constantly under review and restructuring; it would become archaic and ineffective if it wasn't.

By the mid-1970s the system of 'unit beat policing' had well and truly arrived: Lifton was the sole remaining station open in the north of the Tavistock sub-division, while Yelverton, with its sergeant, had taken over responsibility for all the smaller stations in the south of the area. Transport at this time, incidentally, included motorcycles, Ford Escort 'panda cars' (so named because of their distinctive blue and white livery) and mini-vans. In fact, the mini-van at Tavistock played a vital role in many aspects of the life of the community, one of them, on a somewhat lighter note, being connected with a certain problem ...

The station's inspector at the time that the mini-van was introduced was a keen member of the local cricket club, and the problem was that the ground was prone to ponies and sheep wandering off the moors and onto the pitch, causing damage and a nuisance. Some ingenious scheme had to be thought of to keep the livestock off the pitch, and the inspector soon found the answer – tiger dung! Now tiger dung, as anyone will tell you, is a potent and effective material when it comes to frightening sheep and ponies. One can only suppose that in the mind of a sheep "where there's tiger dung, there must be a tiger!". So, the police mini-van paid a regular visit from Tavistock to Paignton Zoo in order to collect large quantities of the required material. It is reported that it was highly successful and kept livestock away from Tavistock cricket pitch for as long as the inspector stayed in post, which is probably why they now use a plain and simple electric fence!

While progressing to meet the urgency of police work and the demands of the public, it was still realised that the public missed their local constable, with his extensive knowledge of the community and friendly face. As a result, in 1978 the then Chief Constable, Mr John Alderson, introduced a system of community policing, and Yelverton was issued with a cycle for its first new style community constable, Gerry Falvey. At the same time Constable Dick Hancock of Tavistock, who was a well-known figure on the streets, took over the town beat with his cycle (he was later to be replaced by Constable Trevor Masters, whose family were local Tavistock people), while the rural villages were allocated to other constables as areas of responsibility, to visit regularly and to get to know people on their new beats. In addition, these constables still had to cover the emergency response car, so it was, in effect, a compromise between leaving the local officer in the community as well as ensuring the police could respond quickly by radio car when urgent matters arose.

The community constables of Tavistock, Lifton and Yelverton are positions which are still filled to ensure that the close relationship between police and public is maintained. The constable on his cycle in the villages was, undoubtedly, a popular and, subsequently, a greatly missed figure, but he could not get to urgent calls as quickly as his successors now can. He was not equipped to deal with the more mobile criminal travelling many miles to commit his offences throughout the whole of the West Devon area. So, regrettably, change had to come. It is true that many constables were as discontented about this change as the public, but the last 20 years have shown that the police of Tavistock and West Devon could not have effectively served the area had it not been for that progress.

Of course, no sooner does the present moment pass by, than it becomes history. So, too, must the police service accept that if we were to stand still and not change to meet the demands of society, then society itself would leave us behind. That, needless to say, is never likely to happen and, indeed, as recently as 1996, the public demands for an ever more mobile police force were met by the centralisation of the telephone calls system to the West Devon stations. This meant that even during the periods when the local enquiry office was closed, a call could be answered and a problem discussed. Nowadays, the West Devon area is also covered 24 hours a day by response vehicles from Tavistock. With support from their community constable colleagues and detective officers, they provide the backbone of policing that has changed to meet the demands and expectations of society.

Computerisation has revolutionised the speedier tasking of officers to emergencies. Criminal records are examined locally at Tavistock station, whereas this would have taken days of researching at Exeter or Bristol. Tavistock, like all other stations in the two counties, is involved in the taking of D.N.A. samples from offenders – something which would have been as unbelievable to the likes of Superintendent Mitchell, as a man walking on the moon. Resources and other support are close at hand. With the city of Plymouth not far away, help can be obtained at little notice, whether it be a police dog or traffic patrol unit; the radio effectively makes West Devon a much smaller place for emergency police response. Tavistock, because of its close proximity to Dartmoor, also makes great use of the police helicopter. Stationed at Exeter, it is little more than 15 minutes flying time away and available to attend any incident. Whether it be involved in a moorland search for a missing person or tracking a stolen car through the winding lanes of West Devon, it has served its purpose time and time again. The police helicopter is also called upon countless times to evacuate injured motorists to hospital following accidents, something that could mean the difference between life and death given that the narrow roads of the area make the task of land ambulances very difficult, especially during the summer months.

Another indication of the positive effects of progress is to be found in the relationship that has developed over many years between the police

'Le Bobbie Anglais' confusing French motorists! (Rue de Napoleon I, Pontivy) 1993.

Author's collection

stations of Tavistock and its twin town of Pontivy in Britany, France. Nowadays exchange visits take place every year and a variety of challenges are presented to visiting officers. Such events usually include attempts at directing each other's traffic circulation, which may be a rather amusing sight for the locals, but one that also demonstrates pride in the service. Tavistock has also played host to other police officers from all corners of the world – from America, Italy and even south east Asia and Russia. Moreover, when the Devon & Cornwall Constabulary receive international guests, it is often Tavistock that is used to describe the ancient traditions of the British policing structure, for it is a showpiece, traditional police station which the force is proud to use to great effect in describing to our foreign colleagues how our policing system is so successful.

Even the internal layout of the police station, itself, goes through periods of redevelopment. Offices are changed to meet new requirements and the interior of the building is altered accordingly. The exterior, however, is protected. A photograph taken nowadays on a Sunday morning without cars is practically identical to one taken over a hundred years ago when Superintendent Merritt first walked out of his new station. Little, for certain, will change in years to come – the police station and guildhall will surely remain one of the lasting images of this special town.

❋ ❋ ❋ ❋ ❋

EPILOGUE

(The End of an Era?)

Any work which purports to be an account of ongoing historical fact can never be finished, for when does history end and the future commence? This work was never intended as some definitive history of the policing of Tavistock and West Devon, nor was it written by an experienced author. It was, instead, simply put together by a policeman of Tavistock, like one of the many mentioned herein, whose commitment to the area is, hopefully, reflected in these pages. It is an account of celebration, a celebration of service for 150 years. Much has had to be left out, and to those many officers whose names have been forgotten through the passage of time, I offer my apologies. They can, however, rest assured that their quiet contribution has been significant to this story and to the success of those who followed them.

Space in such a small book might not have permitted every account to be retold, but that does not detract from the importance of everything that has been repeated during my researches. Is this an "account of an end of an era of policing?", I was asked many times. "Certainly not" is the answer, for when does an era or generation end?

Researching this story has brought to life memories of things gone past that many of us think of as anecdotes on a piece of paper. But to the old men of the Devon Constabulary still able to recall incidents as vividly as yesterday, these are not forgotten parts of history; they are as fresh and relevant now as the day they took place. How our policing ancestors coped with much of what they dealt with, without the modern-day resources and counselling that present-day officers take for granted, is remarkable. Like the soldiers of the trenches, they were not allowed to suffer the traumas of what they saw and dealt with. Instead, they were told to just swallow hard and "get on with it". They suffered deprivation and hardships that would be intolerable in a modern-day police service, more often than not without complaint. It is their sense of duty and commitment that is worn so proudly in the uniforms of the police officers of today. For it was upon their efforts and dedication that the image of the British police system was created. It is to those police officers of yesterday that a debt of gratitude is owed, for we officers of today could not rightly wear our uniforms so proudly were it not for them. If this small book repays some of that debt, then it was worth writing.

❉ ❉ ❉ ❉ ❉

APPENDIX I

Notable Dates

A thumbnail sketch of events in the police service, both nationally and locally, is provided for interest and reference. It is by no means intended as a definitive catalogue of every aspect of policing, or its history:-

870– The reign of Alfred the Great, during which an effective system
899 of mutual pledging existed.
1066 The Norman Conquest, after which the Anglo-Saxon system fell into disuse.
1166 'The Assize of Clarendon' whereby Henry II reaffirmed mutual pledging.
1181 'The Assize of Arms'. Every freeman had to bear arms for preserving the peace and securing criminals and, when necessary, to raise the 'hue and cry'.
1195 Richard I appointed knights to assist in the maintenance of law and order. These were later known as 'Conservators of the Peace' and later 'Justices of the Peace'.
1252 Term 'constable' was used for the first time.
1285 'The Statute of Winchester'. The police system of Edward I based upon the Hundred, the use of the 'hue and cry' and 'watch and ward' was created.
1344 Conservators of the Peace were given judicial functions.
1360 The title 'Justice of the Peace' first used. Their powers were enlarged.
1600 About this time the 'Tithing' system disappeared and was replaced by Justices and constables.
1655 Cromwell's system of military policing arrived.
1673 Justices were empowered to appoint constables.
1748 Henry Fielding became a London police magistrate.
1792 The 'Middlesex Justices Acts' established new police magistrates offices.
1829 Metropolitan Police formed by Sir Robert Peel.
1831 The 'Special Constables Act'.
1833 The 'Lighting and Watching Act'. Parishes were empowered to elect inspectors and appoint watchmen.

1835 The 'Municipal Corporations Act'. Every borough was required to appoint a 'watch committee' with a duty of maintaining a police force.

1837 Superintendent Merritt appointed in charge of Tavistock Parish Police.

1839 Justices in quarter sessions were empowered to establish police forces in counties.

1842 John Physick appointed as deputy for Superintendent Merritt.
Act of Parliament setting conditions of service for parish constables.

1844 Constabulary Almanac published detailing Tavistock's parish police.

1845 Tavistock Parish Police force appointed seven constables.

1846 Bere Alston parish started to pay its parish constables.

1848 Tavistock's new police station guildhall opened on 28th September.
Whitchurch parish force increased from two to three constables.

1849 Tavistock parish force increased to ten constables.

1850 John Crossman appointed as third paid officer for Tavistock police.

1851 Tavistock parish force was increased to eleven constables.

1856 The 'County and Borough Police Act'. The establishment of police forces in every borough and county was made compulsory. The appointment of 'Her Majesty's Inspectors of Constabulary' was created.
Devon Constabulary created.

1857 Devon Constabulary arrived in Tavistock in November.
Superintendent Benjamin Hill appointed in charge of 'K' division.
Sergeant Connell and Constable Ireland were dismissed from service.

1864 Superintendent William Pickford replaced Superintendent Hill.

1875 Superintendent William Cornwall replaced Superintendent Pickford.

1876 New style pickelhaub helmets were introduced.

1877 (2nd September) 2nd Class Constable 4 John Deacon at Milton Abbot was locked up for being drunk and disorderly and assault.

1878 (10th January) 1st Class Constable 277 Elias Gorman was moved from Lewdown station.
(16th August) Superintendent William Mitchell arrived in Tavistock from Barnstaple and took over from Superintendent Cornwall.
(17th October) 1st Class Constable 324 William Parr was at Princetown.
(27th November) The Horrabridge railway fatality witnessed by Superintendent Mitchell.
(9th December) Sergeant Richards was stationed at Tavistock.
(25th December) 1st Class Constable 291 William Gillard at Bere Town died.

1878 (29th December) 1st Class Constable 126 John Clarke was removed from Mary Tavy to Bere Town and 1st Class Constable 324 William Parr was moved from Princetown to Mary Tavy.

1879 (January) Constables Garland and Whimple were in the Tavistock section area, 1st Class Constable Cardew was at Milton Abbot.

(March 15th) 2nd Class Constable 327 John Howard at Bridestowe died.

Sergeant Cooksley at Lifton was in charge of Chillaton station.

Constable Labdon of Chillaton went by train to Tavistock to report sick.

1880 1st Class Constable Cardew of Milton Abbot recommended for promotion.

1881 Constable Martin was at Broadwoodwidger.

Constable Parr was moved from Tavistock to Broadwoodwidger.

2nd Class Constable Glandfield was moved from Lifton to Tavistock (he lived in lodgings as he was a single man).

Constable Labdon was removed from Chillaton to Lifton.

Constable Simpson at Tavistock was to live in one of the police houses at rear of the station.

Constable Wilson (a single man) was removed from Tavistock.

(2nd November) 'Chimney Sweeps Act' was imposed at Tavistock.

Sergeant Holland was at Lifton, with Constables Cardew at Milton Abbot and Kemp at Mary Tavy.

1882 (January) Staff in Lifton section include 1st Class Sergeant Stapleton, 1st Class Constables Parr, Westacott, Gorman, and 2nd Class Constable Kelly.

(September) Removals – 2nd Class Constable Yelland from Princetown to Mary Tavy, 1st Class Constable 8 James Vanstone from Lamerton to Princetown and 2nd Class Constable Chane from Tavistock to Lamerton.

(December 27th) Affray at Princetown with railway navvies. Constable Vanstone was injured. Constable Simpson & Sergeant Richards went to help.

1883 (January) Two constables recommended for Princetown station.

Railway opening in the summer at Princetown and a second constable was needed. Suggestion of posting the Lifton man there temporarily.

1884 (March 9th) 2nd Class Constable James Cleane of Lamerton died.

1885 (January 6th) 'Riot Act' read in Tavistock and 12 extra constables in the town. Problems with disorderly miners.

(November 11th) Bratton Clovelly – Constable Edford caught with Liberal Party poster in window of his police house.

1886 (July 10th) Election riots. Superintendent Collins arrived and commanded force of officers, including Sergeant Coles.

(December) Constable Jones at Horrabridge was stabbed.

1888 Sergeant Stapleton and Constable Guscott were at Tavistock.
Constable Bright was moved from Morwellham to Tavistock.
Constable Ediford was moved from Tavistock to Morwellham.
Constable Parker at Tavistock had posting delayed because his wife was expecting a baby.

1889 Constable Jones at Horrabridge exchanged with Constable Bright at Morwellham.
Superintendent Mitchell complimented the 'H' division men at Plymouth races on their appearance.
(October) Removal for four months of Constable Simpson from Chillaton to Bratton Clovelly and the Bratton Clovelly man, Constable Avent, was removed to Bere Alston because of railway navvy problems.
Request for extra men for Tavistock due to the navvy problems.
Constable Lang was moved from Milton Abbot to Tavistock.

1890 Murder at Bannawell Street.
Constable Avent removed from Bere Alston to Chillaton (he was extra staff at Bere Alston).
Accommodation was being sought at Lydford junction for a constable (the village station was unsuitable).
Removals – Constable Perkins from Lifton to Bratton Clovelly and Constable Bibbings from Lydford to Broadwoodwidger.
(July 17th) Great flood at Tavistock station.
Prisoners transported to Lifton and Stonehouse, and officers sent away into lodgings.
Joseph Denny was arrested for breaking into Dartmoor Prison.
Constable Callard was summonsed for trespass at Lamerton.

1891 Request from magistrates for cells not to be used.
1st Class Constable Richard Bright unfit for duty through injury, he fell off Prisoner Denny's cart at Princetown.
(April) Allegation of child murdered at workhouse by the mother.
Constable Newman was moved from Lifton to Lydford junction and Constable Shutler was moved from Lydford to Tavistock.
Request for Princetown station water supply. The constable had to go some distance to carry water.
(May) Recommendation made for 1st Class Constable 91 W. Cardew at Princetown for promotion to sergeant at Lifton (with 26 years service).
Ex-Constable John Simpson died at Tavistock.
(November 18th) Closure of Morwellham station.
Constable Crispin left Morwellham and went to Princetown as Constable Cardew was retiring.
Constable Guscott removed from Lewdown to Tavistock, and Constable Melhuish was moved from Lifton to Lewdown.

1892 (July) Superintendent Mitchell retired from Tavistock and

Superintendent Nicholls took over.

1892 New cells built and repairs to station made in September.
Removals – Constable Andrews from Bridestowe to Tavistock, Constable Holwill from Tavistock to Bridestowe, Constable Filmore from Whitchurch to Chillaton, Constable Cole from Chillaton to Tavistock, and a request for a recruit to be posted to Whitchurch was made.
(16th November) Double murder at Peter Tavy.
(November) Removals – Constable 300 Yelland from Mary Tavy to Bere Alston and Constable Melhuish to swap.

1893 (January) Constable Callard left Lamerton for elsewhere. Suggestion made that Constable 275 George Lang should move from Tavistock to Lamerton.
Milton Abbot and Lydford stations moved into the Lifton beat.

1903 Superintendent Gordon replaced Superintendent Nicholls.

1904 Bush hats took over from helmets.

1907 The helmet returns.

1921 Tavistock ceased to be a divisional headquarters (transferred to Crownhill).

1922 Lamerton beat closed and transferred to Whitchurch beat.

1932 Dartmoor Prison mutiny.

1936 Programme of building new police houses in villages commenced.

1953 New police station built at Princetown.

1958 Tavistock police social club opened.

1964 Lydford station closed in August and beat amalgamated into Mary Tavy beat.
New stations opened at Lifton and Yelverton.

1966 Ladycross beat went over to Cornwall County Constabulary.

1967 Devon and Cornwall County Constabularies amalgamated to form the Devon & Cornwall Constabulary.

1971 Milton Abbot station closed.
Mary Tavy station closed.
Bere Alston station closed.

1978 Introduction of 'community policing'.

1979 Tavistock police station was expanded when Social Services vacated the building.

1994 Princetown station closed.

1996 (1st April) Lifton and Yelverton stations closed.
Tavistock police social club closed.

1997 150th Anniversary of Tavistock police station.

✳ ✳ ✳ ✳ ✳

APPENDIX II

WHAT'S IN A NUMBER?

(The Development of the Shoulder Number)

The Devon & Cornwall Constabulary, formed in 1967, is made up from an amalgamation of four old police forces – The Devon County Constabulary, the Cornwall County Constabulary, the Plymouth City Police and the Exeter City Police. Up until the amalgamations, one could find an officer with the same shoulder number in each of those four constabularies.

The first two forces to merge were the old Devon County Constabulary and the Exeter City Police, in 1966; this resulted in the formation of the new Devon & Exeter Police. Although the Devon & Exeter Police existed for only about 18 months, this was an important step in the first phase of amalgamations in the police throughout the counties of Devon and Cornwall.

At that time the Devon Constabulary consisted of less than 600 men, so they had shoulder numbers to a maximum of three figures. It was decided to allow the former Devon Constabulary officers to retain their numbers when their constabulary merged with the Exeter City force, while the old Exeter City Police shoulder numbers simply had 900 added to them to make them into new Devon & Exeter Police numbers. This then avoided any possible duplication with the old Devon numbers.

It was, therefore, easy to see which men had been in the former Devon or Exeter forces just by looking at their shoulders. For the first time an officer serving in the old Exeter City Police might end up having a four-figure shoulder number, if his original number had been 100 or more, because of adding 900 to it.

In 1967 the second phase of amalgamations took place when the Devon & Exeter Police combined with the Plymouth City Police and Cornwall County Constabulary to create the new Devon & Cornwall Constabulary. Another shoulder number change was therefore necessary, again so as to avoid duplication. After all, the same number might still be found on officers from the Devon & Exeter Police, The Plymouth City Police and the Cornwall County Constabulary.

As a result, it was decided that 1100 would be added to the Plymouth City shoulder numbers to make them into new Devon & Cornwall ones.

One example was when Constable 91 Samuel Foden of the Plymouth City Police became Constable 1191 of the newly created Devon & Cornwall Constabulary.

Likewise, Cornwall numbers also changed, but in a little less rigid manner it seems – approximately 1600 was added to the old Cornwall Constabulary numbers. In this instance it was a fairly loose rule, and a few minor adjustments were made to avoid duplication Therefore an ex-Cornwall Constabulary number, in some instances, made a new Devon & Cornwall number that could be higher than 2000.

These changes were bound to be unpopular amongst some of the officers who were not keen on the amalgamations, and resistance occurred in a few areas. Indeed, it was to be many years before the old individually unique uniforms of the four constituent forces were eventually cast aside by their somewhat 'aged and devoted' owners, and true uniformity was eventually achieved! (Even as late as the 1970s, the old Cornwall Constabulary uniform was still to be seen, worn by some of the older officers of the county).

Once the amalgamation had been completed by the end of 1967, new recruits to the force were issued with the shoulder numbers of officers who had recently retired, thus relinquishing their numbers. It therefore became possible to identify from which of the old forces the re-issued shoulder number came. Officers often enquired keenly as to the history of their number, and many traced the ancestry of their own individual number through generations of officers.

It was realised, however, that just re-issuing old shoulder numbers would not take into account, or keep up with, the level of recruiting into the Devon & Cornwall Constabulary, which at that time exceeded the rate of retirements. A new numbering system had to be devised to take into account this increase in establishment, and for some time it had been felt that shoulder numbers of Devon & Cornwall officers should be standardised. The old established system of re-issuing retiring officers' shoulder numbers to new recruits was to be phased out, although it did carry on for a few years, alongside a new system of issuing brand new numbers. For example, new numbers as high as 2363 were issued for the first time as early as 1973, whilst some old, retired officers' lower numbers continued to be re-issued after that date.

This meant that a new recruit could be issued with a shoulder number less than a colleague with far greater seniority in service, although to many it didn't seem to matter at the time. An example of the re-issuing of an old number was when Constable Samuel Foden, mentioned earlier, formerly Constable 91 of the old Plymouth City Police, retired in 1976. Until his retirement he carried his new style Devon & Cornwall Constabulary number 1191 on his shoulder, following the 1967 amalgamations. His shoulder number was simply re-issued the following year, in the May of 1977, to a new recruit – by chance, the author!

(Samuel's own son, Michael, like many mentioned within this book, became a policeman and served for several years at Tavistock and Yelverton).

The last number to be re-issued from a retired officer was in 1980. From that date all new Devon & Cornwall Constabulary recruits were issued with their own new unique shoulder numbers, bearing no historical relationship to any of the four constituent former police forces, which make up the Devon & Cornwall Constabulary.

Those officers who had joined the force and had been given an old re-issued number simply retained that number, and, because these were never consecutive, they gave no clues as to the length of service of the officer. These old style numbers will eventually be lost, never to be re-issued, when their 'owners' retire, and so yet another aspect of the force will ultimately pass into the history books. The new system of issuing only consecutive numbers commenced with 2509, and from that time, in the early 1980s, this has remained the pattern.

By now the highest number on a police officer's shoulder in the Devon & Cornwall Constabulary is over 4000, and it looks likely to exceed 5000 by the year 2000.

So just look next time you see a police officer greet a colleague and see where they look first – it will invariably be at the shoulder number. For it is only on the shoulders of constables and sergeants that any clue will be found as to the length of service of the bearer. If the number should be less than 2509, however, one can only take a guess and assume you are talking to 'an old sweat'!

Inspectors and above do not display their numbers on their uniforms; they show their badges of rank instead. They do, however, retain their shoulder numbers when promoted, for identification purposes, especially in today's computer age when police officers of whatever rank are only recognised by their own individually unique number.

The custom of referring to an identification number as a 'collar number' is a rather more curious oddity retained by many of the old stalwarts of the force. This is a throw back to the time, often regarded as the halcyon days of policing, when high-necked tunics were worn with the identification number on the collar. (Incidentally, from the last few years of Queen Victoria's reign, the Devon Constabulary wore only a crown on their collars; with their identification numbers and divisional letter being displayed on their shoulder epaulettes, unlike most other forces which retained numbers on their collars).

This is all part of the rich tapestry of the history of the police service – and long may that tradition continue!

❋ ❋ ❋ ❋ ❋

BIBLIOGRAPHY

A History of the Police in England & Wales, T. A. Critchley (published privately, 1967)

Devon Constabulary – Chief Constable's Headquarters circulations 1876 to 1889 (internal circulars)

Morwellham Quay – A History, Amber Patrick (Morwellham Quay Museum, 1990)

Of constables and peelers, Gerry Woodcock (unpublished notes, 1995)

Out of the Blue (a history of the Devon Constabulary 1856 to 1956), Walter J. Hutchings (The Devon Constabulary, 1957)

Out of the Blue II, Kenneth J. Mallett (unpublished notes of the history of the Devon Constabulary 1956 to 1967, 1968)

Police correspondence book of Tavistock 'K' Divisional Headquarters, 1875 to 1894 (unpublished)

Police diary and occurrence book of Constable Trigger of Mary Tavy station, 1911 to 1913 (unpublished)

Sherbourne and Yeovil Mercury, 1848

Tavistock Abbey – A study in the Social and Economic History of Devon, H. P. R. Finberg (David & Charles, 1969)

Tavistock's Yesterdays (Vol. 9), Gerry Woodcock (published privately, 1993)

The Horrabridge Beat Book (Police occurrence book of the Horrabridge station, 1923 to 1968) (unpublished)

The Mary Tavy Beat Book (Police occurrence book of the Mary Tavy station, 1919 to 1966) (unpublished)

The Tamar Journals (Vol. 16), an article entitled 'The Strikes at Devon Great Consols', Gerry Woodcock (*The Tamar Journals*, 1968)

Walkhampton – Church, Parish and Village, L. Govier (published privately, 1984)

✳ ✳ ✳ ✳ ✳

THE AUTHOR

Although born in Middlesex, Simon Dell came to Bideford in North Devon as a young schoolboy with a burning desire – like many boys of that age – to be a policeman. Later, whilst still attending school, he developed a passion for Dartmoor and then decided that not only did he still want to become a policeman, but to become a Tavistock policeman!

Eventually, after leaving school in 1975, Simon's ambition was partially realised when he joined the Devon & Cornwall Constabulary as a cadet, based in Exeter. He then became a constable two years later and, in 1981, saw his ambition fulfilled in its entirety – he was posted to Tavistock. Shortly afterwards he also joined the local section of the Dartmoor Rescue Group, subsequently becoming the group's chairman. Meanwhile, in 1985, Simon became the town's community constable, a position that he was to occupy for no less than 11 years. During that period he received various accolades for his style of policing, in addition to being awarded the 'Ada Murrin' cup for community policing (1990) and being made 'Citizen of the Year' (1991). Of even greater significance, he received two Chief Constable's commendations for bravery, one for the arrest of a man with a loaded pistol!

Simon, who was included in the New Year's Honours List of 1997 and presented with the M.B.E. by the Queen for services to the community, both through his policing and rescue work on Dartmoor, is currently the divisional training officer for the East Cornwall division, based at Launceston. At other times, when not on duty, he is involved with various voluntary and youth organisations, and enjoys nothing better than a walk on Dartmoor with his border collie, Sam.

Although now working outside the immediate area, Simon still lives in Tavistock with his wife, Shirley, and their two children, Matthew and Laura, and he has never lost sight of that burning ambition that brought him to the town. Perhaps one day, who knows, he might achieve that same ambition again and walk *The Beat on Western Dartmoor*!

Simon Dell, MBE